IN THE LONG RUN WE'RE ALL DEAD

IN THE LONG RUN WE'RE ALL DEAD

THE LIVES AND DEATHS OF GREAT ECONOMISTS

BJÖRN FRANK

Translated from German by Jamie Bulloch

First published in 2023 by
Haus Publishing Ltd
4 Cinnamon Row
London SW11 3TW

Copyright © Berenberg Verlag, Berlin 2019
English-language copyright © Jamie Bulloch, 2023

A CIP catalogue for this book is available from the British Library

ISBN 978-1-913368-57-9
eISBN 978-1-913368-58-6

Typeset in Garamond by MacGuru Ltd
Printed in the UK by Clays

www.hauspublishing.com
@HausPublishing

The translation of this work was supported by a grant from the Goethe-Institut

 GOETHE INSTITUT

Contents

When I hear that there's a four-volume Shaw biography
running to 2,000 pages I say, Thanks my dear friend,
that's a meticulous piece of work, but couldn't you have
got to the point more quickly by leaving things out?

Hans Magnus Enzensberger

Every biography is a novel that dares not speak its name.

Roland Barthes

About This Book and Why it's Not Longer

On 9 June 2013, the Swedish biochemist Alf Stefan Andersson, professor at the University of Houston, was battered to death by his girlfriend with her stiletto heel. *That's one way for an academic to get into the papers*, I thought at the time. But a pointless one – it was a news item, not a story, and it certainly didn't teach you anything about biochemistry.

I thought of the economists whose lives were worthy of fiction, as if some novelist had dreamed up not only how they lived, but how they died too. Whether they killed themselves, were killed, faked their death, or died miserably from a disease, it always seemed to be linked to their work. This is true of Jeremy Bentham, for example, who advocated 'the greatest happiness of the greatest number', thereby laying the philosophical foundation stone of economic science. And of Friedrich List, who fought for free trade as well as protective tariffs and the development of the railways. It's also true of John Maynard Keynes, the aesthete amongst economists. I didn't want to write potted biographies of these people; I wanted to tell stories ending in a death that illuminates their life and work.

When you read this book, I don't mind if you ask, 'Is that really true?' In each case the answer is 'yes', because I've made nothing up. At most, I've been slightly selective, but everything in these pages is true and substantiated by evidence (well, almost everything – it's easy to spot the few passages where I've had to veer into speculation and use my imagination). I've set myself one further rule: a quirky death alone doesn't justify a subject's inclusion. All the economists who appear in this book are important. Some, like John von Neumann, were geniuses of their time. Others, such as Joseph Alois Schumpeter, were the instigators of entire fields of research. Yet others have been immortalised by giving their names to laws or phenomena – like Richard Cantillon (the 'Cantillon Effect').

As I was writing, I often thought about how, in the early 1980s, young tennis players like me made ourselves look ridiculous when serving. Standing with one foot behind the other and both parallel to the baseline, we were trying to emulate John McEnroe, as was plain for all to see. My role model for this book may not be so easy to spot: he is the McEnroe of biographical writing, Lytton Strachey. Both men are clearly geniuses, enfants terribles in the eyes of their contemporaries, and it's impossible to imitate them. Strachey makes a brief appearance in one chapter as the lover of a very famous economist. Far more importantly, however, he showed that a biography need not be solemn in tone; it can be ironic too. This is even true in the face of his very own tragedy. Terminally ill with stomach cancer, Strachey uttered his last words:

'If this is dying, then I don't think much of it.' His partner, the painter Dora Carrington, unable to get over his death, shot herself. She was thirty-eight; he was fifty-one. Statistically they are both outriders, especially Carrington, for on average authors die significantly earlier than painters or other artists, which is presumably down to the fact that authors seldom have contact with the public. They spend years writing a book and only very rarely experience the satisfaction of having come up with something decent. For authors, moreover, the process of producing their work is joyless in comparison to the experiences of actors and musicians, who rehearse and perform together with other creatives. Painting, also a lonely pursuit, at least speaks to various senses and can be undertaken in a variety of locations. If a writer makes up for the sad activity at his or her desk by extreme behaviour in their free time, it is not exactly beneficial to health or life expectancy.

I've tried to take these insights seriously. None of my chapters are longer than they need to be. There are enough voluminous biographies around as it is. In addition, I've attempted to avoid writing in total isolation. For example, I've read chapters out to people and sent them off as early as possible. The number of people who made me feel that I'd already crafted a finished product, even when it was only a fifth of a book, is so great that I couldn't possibly draw up a list of names here.

I am especially grateful for the encouragement from those who couldn't care less about economics and wouldn't read about it otherwise. This book is written for them.

1

Cantillon's Last Problem

RICHARD CANTILLON
1680–1734

What to do with your time when you're dead, when you've departed the world you were used to living in? Embark on something new? Catch up on something you've missed? Richard Cantillon, we know for certain, wrote a book about the economy – a real book, not an ethereal whisper from the graveyard, but a volume that was printed in 1755, twenty-one years after his death.

All of this might have been forgotten, had the British economist and philosopher William Stanley Jevons not rediscovered the book and paid tribute to it in the *Contemporary Review* in 1881. As Jevons observed in a footnote, this was made easier by the fact that he'd 'found' one of the few surviving copies in his private library, after having 'accidentally bought' it in Paris many years earlier.

As well as congratulating Jevons on his discovery, we should also pay respect to his disciplined reading – the book is really heavy going. The three chapters that make the most significant contribution to monetary theory are entitled 'On the increase and decrease in the quantity of hard money in a state', 'Continuation of the same subject of the increase and decrease in the quantity of hard money in a state', and 'Further reflection on the same subject of the increase and decrease in the quantity of hard money in a state'. What the author describes on these pages is now known as the Cantillon Effect, and it is not merely of historical interest. The effect keeps occurring even today, as a result of the Greek or Eurozone crisis.

The European Central Bank (ECB) can only increase the supply of money by making banks lend it more money to provide more credit. Consumers obtain the additional credit to buy more products than before. But what happens if the manufacturers of these products are unable to automatically produce more than before? And what if they don't have a large amount of stock? In such a situation, they only have one sensible response to the rise in demand: they increase the prices.

For a long time, there was little evidence of this. It was puzzling that the ECB's loose monetary policy from 2008 onwards hadn't led to appreciable inflation. Cantillon's analysis helps shed some light on the matter. He wrote his book at a time when the volume of money increased due to new gold or silver mines being opened. But that doesn't happen overnight. The mine is discovered, then the mine owners employ workers, commission smelting companies, and keep a tidy profit for themselves. All these people spend more money than before and truly have become wealthier – because prices are the same, they're able to afford more. But, as Cantillon writes, 'All this increase of expense in meat, wine, wool, etc. diminishes of necessity the share of the other inhabitants of the state who do not participate at first in the wealth of the mines in question,' for now the prices of these goods rise as a result of the increased demand of the mine owners. A general version of this is today understood to be the Cantillon Effect: if the supply of money is increased in a way that first benefits a specific group, this group becomes richer at the expense of other members of the economy. Not only do prices rise as a result, but redistribution takes place too. This process takes time; rather than passing instantly from one hand to another, money moves at a certain speed (which, unlike modern mone-tary theorists, Cantillon doesn't analyse). And not all prices rise uniformly – it begins with the prices of those goods the mine owners and workers want.

What about today? Who spends more once the ECB has raised the money supply? An important group of consumers who finance their acquisitions with credit are property buyers. Anybody who is able to purchase a house at the 'old' price but also benefit from low interest rates has been a real winner from the Eurozone crisis. Those who buy a house in a good location have to pay much more today than at the beginning of the crisis – economists speak of asset price inflation. For some goods, i.e. those that act as an investment, the prices have already risen, whereas they haven't for others. This is the situation described by Cantillon in a new guise.

But there is more to discover in Cantillon. Of particular interest is his population theory. He criticises naive attempts by his contemporaries to describe population growth as simple exponential growth 'from Adam, the first Father'. Although 'men multiply like mice in a barn if they have unlimited means of subsistence', he says, the means are in reality not unlimited. And thus population growth depends on how much the land-owners claim for themselves. The more they take, the less remains for the lower classes, and consequently the state will have fewer inhabitants.

These are thoughts that the Englishman Thomas Robert Malthus later reiterated with a greater degree of consistency, earning him some fame as the man who discovered the 'law of population'. This is a pessimistic theory, according to which all progress in agriculture and every intermittent increase in prosperity results in people having more children, and so, if the calculations are done on a per-capita basis, no gain in the standards of living actually occurs. Whereas broad swathes of the population had little chance to escape destitution, in 1805 Malthus became the first ever professor of economics. Before this, economics was a discipline pursued not at university, but by people who had the necessary time and education to do it. Malthus began as an Anglican curate; Adam Smith, who in 1776 published the classic economics text par excellence, *The Wealth of Nations*, was a philosopher and later earned his money as a private tutor and commissioner of customs; and Cantillon's contemporary François Quesnay was the physician to Madame de Pompadour, Louis XV's mistress.

What about Cantillon himself? His path towards becoming an economist was more obvious: he started out as a banker. Although he was born in a family of Irish farmers between 1680 and 1690 (that's as specific as we can be), his great uncle was an important banker in London and a second cousin took Cantillon on at his bank in Paris, where in 1708 he applied for French citizenship. Eight years later, this cousin narrowly escaped bankruptcy and transferred his now-almost-worthless bank to Cantillon – who had been dealing in wine on the side and earning well from it – for a small annuity.

In 1720 Cantillon turned his bank into a limited partnership called Cantillon & Hughes. John Hughes was his partner and manager, but the other half of the business's name referred not to Richard Cantillon himself but to his four-year-old nephew. Maybe Cantillon designed this set-up to avoid losing more than the capital he had put into the partnership in the case of bankruptcy.

After all, the business he was involved in wasn't without its risks. At the time, Europe was going through one of the most sensational speculation bubbles of all time, concerning shares in the legendary Compagnie du Mississippi. Cantillon didn't purchase any of these shares himself, as he predicted that the bubble would soon burst. But he lent money to investors, mostly English aristocrats, to enable them to buy some. He took these shares as security against the loans but sold most of them immediately, instead of depositing them in his bank. Had the price of these shares continued to rise and his debtors paid back their loans and demanded their shares back, Cantillon would have been in trouble, because he'd have been forced to buy the shares back at a higher price.

But the opposite occurred: the share price plummeted and Cantillon bought back the shares cheaply. Although they belonged to his debtors, they were worth virtually nothing. Nonetheless, they had to pay Cantillon back the money they'd borrowed, together with interest that at times ran as high as 55 per cent. Not all of them accepted this; for years they persisted in filing lawsuits against him for profiteering and fraud. When the aforementioned Hughes died in 1723, his widow sued Cantillon too, for she believed she had a claim to a share of the bank, which he had now liquidated. The legal proceedings dragged out for more than ten years, and Cantillon was involved in several more besides.

No sooner were these resolved than his house in London went up in flames on the night of 14 May 1734. One body was found, so badly burned that it couldn't be identified. It was first suspected that Cantillon had gone to bed to read with a candle, as was his wont – but then a servant who he had dismissed a few days earlier was accused of murder. The suspect was never caught, however.

Here ends the story – or it doesn't. A man who turned up in the Dutch colony of Suriname shortly afterwards with some of Cantillon's papers, and who called himself Chevalier de Louvigny, could have been Cantillon's killer. It may have been coincidental that on the night of his death his wife and daughter were in Paris rather than London, and that before he died he'd withdrawn an unusually large sum of cash from his account. And it's just possible that his posthumous book had been translated into French from the English manuscript, that the original English had been lost, and that the French version had remained unpublished for around twenty years until someone had the idea to print it. But perhaps, in truth, it was Cantillon himself posing behind the guise of the Chevalier, and perhaps Friedrich Melchior, Baron von Grimm, was right when in 1755 he wrote to Denis Diderot:

> For a month we have had a new work on commerce ... entitled *Essai sur la nature du commerce en général, traduit de l'anglais*. The book is not translated from the English as its title leads one to believe. The original work was written in French by an Englishman named Cantillon, a man of standing who ended his days in Languedoc, where he had retired and had lived several years.

In a later letter, however, Melchior retracts this claim and subscribes to the official version. We'll never fully know the true course of events. But if Cantillon did fake his own murder, it was a stroke of genius that at once freed him of all lawsuits and courts. Not one, however, that anybody could know about, or one he could be admired for. But how could he live a life of seclusion and still shine under the name Richard Cantillon? The ploy with his book, arguably the most important work on economics before Adam Smith, worked quite well.

2

Bentham: Not a Pretty Corpse, But Useful

JEREMY BENTHAM
1748–1832

The story that the mortal remains of Jeremy Bentham, sitting on a chair, still take part in the meetings of the senate of University College London almost two centuries after his death, and that the minutes read 'Jeremy Bentham, present but not voting' is a fabrication. No such item exists in the minutes, and the only thing we have reliably on record is that Bentham made an appearance at the 2013 meeting. It's hard to understand the exaggeration; his life and afterlife read so much like a work of fiction that they don't require any further embellishment.

However, Bentham's story is not one of those vulgar, predictable novels in which a character's childhood experiences determine all that comes later. In 1760, at the tender age of twelve, Jeremy Bentham arrived at the Queen's College in Oxford as a child prodigy and was given a room with a view of the graveyard. Nightmares and a fear of ghosts plagued him almost all his life. What became of the traumatised child who left the college at sixteen as a Bachelor of Arts and then studied law? Did he turn into a medium who tried to summon the spirits with all sorts of hocus pocus? Not at all. In Bentham's confrontation with death, his reason took control. When he considered the situation soberly, Bentham found it interesting that he should be afraid of ghosts without believing in them. And in 1769, when he was twenty-one, having just come of age and been licensed as a lawyer, he did something unbelievable: he wrote a will bequeathing his body to medical training and research. This was completely novel at a time when the only bodies you could legally come by for research and for prospective doctors to practise on were those of executed criminals. But science had to wait a long time for Bentham's body.

Bentham's family was so wealthy that he barely needed to work as a lawyer. Instead, he soon made a name for himself as the author of books on law and jurisprudence. And yet his contemporaries knew only a fraction of what he wrote. Bentham often abandoned his manuscripts far too prematurely; much of his writing comes across as rough and disordered. Sometimes he might have had his mind on British politics rather than posterity as he wrote; at other times the problem might have been the speed with which he continually turned to new ideas, deserting half-finished books as Don Juan did broken-hearted women. Most of his works on economics didn't appear until over a century after his death, in a three-volume edition.

Bentham did enough, however, to be regarded as the

undisputed founder of a philosophical school – utilitarianism – although his most famous saying is neither his originally (it was coined by the Italian legal philosopher Cesare Beccaria) nor a useful maxim. It asserts that 'the greatest happiness of the greatest number' is the measure of good government. So what? Should as many people as possible be a little bit happy? Or can a few people be unhappy if a lot are very happy in return? 'The greatest happiness of the greatest number' is about as meaningless as a sporting competition where the aim is to jump both 'as high and as far as possible'. Neither Bentham nor utilitarianism deserve to be saddled with this unfortunate slogan.

Later, Bentham expressed it differently: politics should increase rather than reduce the happiness of citizens. Nowadays that sounds like an obvious demand, but it wasn't in Bentham's time; mercantilism, whose supporters were particularly interested in the influx of precious metals into economies, was coming to an end, and also new was the idea that everybody's happiness should count equally. Until 'yesterday', Bentham wrote in 1821, the world had been ruled by tyrants who cared only about their own happiness.

In the nineteenth century, economics developed in the wake of Bentham's utilitarianism. First, economists adopted the idea that the welfare of a society is nothing other than the welfare of its members. (In contrast to this, there may be goals that an entity like a 'nation', for example, might achieve militarily, without any benefit to its citizens; indeed, it might be to their disadvantage. Economists find things like that strange.) Second, Bentham's ghost hovers over almost every economic model, for he declared that people were constantly working out how to increase their pleasure and reduce their suffering. This sounds like a very simple image of humanity, but it's not. Bentham recognised that there were many different sources of pleasure and suffering – not just sensual pleasure, but the pleasure of friendship, the pleasure of power, the pleasure of imagination, or the pleasure of piety. Then there was the suffering of the senses, the suffering of bad repute, the suffering of memories, the suffering of piety, and so on.

Wealth can provide pleasure directly, but it can also be a means to accessing other pleasures. Like many modern economists, Bentham questioned how material prosperity impacted on happiness. In the absence of illness or any other source of personal unhappiness, the richer of two people should be the happier. Their levels of happiness differ less, however, than their wealth; the richer someone is, the less their happiness increases with each additional thaler, pound, dollar, or euro. Although this is a given for economists today (it is known as 'diminishing marginal utility'), it was a novel idea in Bentham's time, and he went to great lengths to explain it. The reader, he wrote, should imagine 1,000 farmers who had a little more than enough to live on, and then a king who was as rich as all the farmers put together – or, even better, a prince in place of the king, for he would be unencumbered by the burden of ruling. This prince would surely be happier than the average farmer, but not 1,000 times happier. Even if he were only five or ten times happier, that would be remarkable, Bentham wrote.

If money brings more happiness to the poor than to the rich, it must logically follow that overall happiness would be at its greatest if everyone had the same amount. And Bentham indeed came to this conclusion – which doesn't mean he thought that money should be taken from the rich until all differences between rich and poor had disappeared. On the one hand, nobody would bother to increase their wealth, as whatever they earned would be immediately taken from them. On the other hand, happiness depends not only on how much money you have but how you have ended up with that amount. Money that is gained increases happiness, but if the same amount is lost the impact on happiness is greater (and, of course, negative).

As with all eighteenth- and nineteenth-century economists, the source of such psychological insight was merely intro-spection, or at best everyday observation. Since the 1980s, however, numerous experiments have shown that Bentham was right. The economists Jack Knetsch and Jack Sinden, for example, divided some students into two groups. To the first group they gave lottery tickets, and offered to buy them back for $2. Exactly half of the students took them up on this offer; the other half elected to keep their tickets. The other group was given the option to purchase a lottery ticket for $2. Only a quarter of these were willing to do so. The lottery ticket was clearly more desirable, therefore, to the students who already possessed one, and this group found it hard to part with. In other words, the feelings of those who have the ticket and sell it must on average be stronger than the feelings of those who purchase one. Loss has a greater impact on happiness than acquisition.

Knetsch carried out a similar experiment together with two men who would later become Nobel laureates in Economics: Daniel Kahneman, a psychologist who won in 2002, and Richard Thaler, the 2017 winner. The three researchers gave some students a Cornell University coffee mug, which they had the option of keeping or selling as they wished. Unaware of the price of the mug, the participants were quoted a number of different figures and asked whether they would sell for that sum. The remaining students who weren't given a mug had the opportunity to purchase one. The average price the buyers were willing to pay was $2.45, whereas those who owned the mugs valued them far higher, at an average of $5.50. The very fact of possessing something makes it seem more valuable to us – a frequently observed phenomenon, known as the 'endowment effect'.

That Bentham intuitively grasped what economists proved by experiment almost two centuries later helped him to answer the following question: what is the actual damage that a thief causes? Or, more precisely: what is the economic damage? The victim is poorer, but the thief is richer by the same amount. Doesn't that simply mean that income has been redistributed within an economy? Admittedly, if there's been a break-in involving a smashed window, a blown safe, or a poisoned guard dog, then it's obvious that the victim has lost more than the thief has gained. But Bentham was the first economist who clearly understood that even pickpocketing causes damage – not material damage to the economy, but a loss of happiness, because the loss inflicts more pain on the victim than the gain causes pleasure to the thief.

What should be done, therefore, to reduce the incidence of stealing? Bentham's answer is characteristic of his entire way of thinking. It is quite obvious, he argued, that the pleasure a thief obtains from stealing outweighs his suffering from the act. Thus the pleasure must be reduced and the suffering increased. This is the justification for punishing thieves.

In Bentham's time, prisons truly were places of suffering. Inmates, locked up in damp and cold dungeons, were at the mercy of incompetent and sometimes brutal guards. Poorly nourished and occasionally chained up, they wasted away, barely able to perform the forced labour imposed on them. This wasn't the sort of punishment Bentham envisaged. If prisons had to exist, they ought to be far more useful!

Bentham's decades-long dream of extensive prison reform began in 1786. Undertaking the biggest journey of his life, he visited Russia, where his brother Samuel was in the service of Grigory Potemkin (yes, the very same adviser to, and ex-lover of, Catherine the Great, and the man who gave his name to the Potemkin villages). Samuel Bentham was an engineer; he helped Potemkin with the economic exploitation and military protection of large territories in the Tsarist empire. When Jeremy arrived, Samuel was building riverboats to transport construction material from Potemkin's property in Krychaw (now in Belarus) to the Black Sea via the Sozh and the Dnieper.

Although there was no lack of money, the manpower that Samuel needed simply didn't exist locally, so he got Englishmen to come over to train and supervise the Russian workers. It soon transpired, however, that amongst those who left England to seek their fortune in 'White Russia' were a handful of problematic characters in need of supervising themselves. Samuel planned, therefore, a central viewing platform around which the various work crews, separated by wooden fences, could be arranged like slices of a cake. There was to be a sort of pavilion on the platform that wasn't easily visible from outside. The structure was never built, because Potemkin sold his property and gave Samuel other tasks to get on with. Jeremy, however, was hooked, and he developed Samuel's idea into a completely new type of prison: the panopticon. It was round, with a tower in the middle from which an inspector had a view of all the cells, without the prisoners (and the guards under the inspector) knowing whether they were being monitored at any particular moment. For one thing, this is efficient. Although it's impossible to observe all the prisoners at the same time, each individual prisoner has to assume they're under permanent supervision and behave accordingly.

Bentham had high expectations with regard to the effect it would have on prisoners: 'Morals reformed – health preserved – industry invigorated – public burthens [*sic*] lightened … all by a simple idea in architecture!'

The panopticon gave rise to a wealth of ingenious analyses by professional Bentham interpreters. Some saw in Bentham's psychological naivety – he already imagined himself as the boss of numerous prisons built according to his ideas, which would reform many prisoners – a sign of Asperger's syndrome. Various others regarded him as a reformer who wanted to bring fresh air and running water into the cells; a cool calculator whose only reason for giving prisoners healthy food in sufficient quantities was to enable them to do sixteen hours' work a day; or an intelligent economist who wanted to offer incentives to prison governors – their pay ought to depend on how many inmates survived imprisonment.

We can pick out the bizarre, such as Bentham's idea that the inspector's family should live in the tower too, because at home his wife and children stare pointlessly out of the window, but in the watchtower such behaviour is of practical use. Or we can turn Bentham into the standard-bearer of a philosophical justification for the state that polices and punishes its citizens. The impenetrable volume of literature on the panopticon distorts our vision of Bentham; we see him far more clearly at other places in his biography.

Bentham loved animals, particularly anything with four legs, including the mice that he allowed to run around his study undisturbed. But he also kept The Reverend John Lang-bourne and other cats whose names we don't know – a fact that, as his biographer Leslie Stephen pointed out, was hard to square with the notion of the greatest happiness of the great-est number. Bentham did, however, apply another principle of utilitarianism to animals: because they felt happiness and suffering, their wellbeing was important.

One of the most important utilitarian philosophers of our time, Yew-Kwang Ng, takes Bentham's ideas on animal protect-ion further when seeking to answer whether eating meat is morally acceptable. If we didn't eat chickens, pigs, and cows, most of them wouldn't exist – very few people, for example, would consider keeping an Aberdeen Angus bull as a pet until he died of old age. Is it a good thing, then, that we end up slaughtering and eating large numbers of livestock animals? If we disregard health and environmental issues, Ng believes, it depends on whether the animal's happiness during its lifetime outweighs its suffering. From a utilitarian viewpoint, keeping animals for slaughter is acceptable if the animals have good lives before we eat them.

It could be argued that animals have 'natural rights', but Bentham thought that was 'nonsense on stilts', whether we're talking about animals or people. For him, rights were never naturally given: all rules had to be useful, and all rights had to be justified by the fact that they could increase happiness and reduce suffering. An example can be found in Bentham's arguments for giving women the franchise. He contended that because men cannot know some of women's suffering (such as the strains of pregnancy and the pains of childbirth), their judgement is lacking on issues that relate to women. Or they may have interests that are opposed to those of women; this is true, at least, of men who derive pleasure from hitting their wives. It's a good thing, therefore, for women to represent their own interests.

In the same vein, Bentham argues against colonialism, which he opposed not because the peoples in the colonies had natural rights to independence but because they were better placed than the colonial 'masters' to identify their interests and increase their happiness. He was against the punishment of homosexuals, whose activities clearly gave them pleasure and harmed nobody. He was against the death penalty and in favour of banking regulation, press freedom, and the state playing an active role in education and health. He also proposed the idea of an international court.

Often he tried to go beyond theory and influence politics. For example, he offered his services as the author of progressive legislation to US President James Madison and to Tsar Alexander I. Eventually, Portugal showed some interest, but by the time he'd finally finished his work the liberal revolution there was already history.

One of Bentham's last initiatives would meet with more success. In the 1820s, around seventy-five criminals were being executed per year in the UK, providing far too few bodies for trainee doctors. The institutes bought most of their corpses from the shadowy 'resurrectionists' and asked no questions, because they suspected they were being delivered freshly buried corpses that had been dug up at night. The relatives of the dead didn't have a clue about this, of course. The only person who might know would have been the bribed cemetery-keeper.

In 1826, Bentham sent the British home secretary, Robert Peel, a piece of draft legislation that is reminiscent of the current discourse about organ donorship. Nowadays, some economists suggest rewarding people who fill out a donor card: those who are prepared to donate their organs after their death should be given preference if they need an organ donation themselves, they say. Bentham thought that only patients who would allow their body to be dissected in the event of their death should be treated in hospital. He did not forget to mention his own will in the process:

> So that my last moments have for their comfort the assurance that how little service soever it may have been in my power to render to mankind during my lifetime, I shall at least be not altogether useless after my death.

Although Peel's reply was polite, he preferred not to broach this taboo subject and wished to avoid a public discussion.

Corpses thus remained scarce, and in 1828 two particularly shifty characters in Edinburgh, the 'bodysnatchers' William Burke and William Hare, came up with the idea of sparing themselves the bribe money and strenuous digging. They killed sixteen people before they were caught and themselves ended up on the dissecting table (Burke's skeleton is still preserved today in the Anatomical Museum at the University of Edinburgh). Their activities – and those of a few copycats, who practised 'Burking' too – heightened willingness to return to Bentham's draft law, supported by some influential Bentham devotees in Parliament. The declaration of consent by hospital patients went by the wayside, however; the Anatomy Act of 1832 permitted the dissection of corpses from poorhouses that were unclaimed within forty-eight hours of death by relatives who could afford a burial.

A few weeks before this bill became law, Bentham died at the age of eighty-four. Two days later, on 8 June 1832, friends and select Bentham admirers received an invitation to the opening of his body, undertaken by (and accompanied by a lecture from) his friend Thomas Southwood Smith. Each invitee was allowed to bring another two people along. It's very possible that Bentham's friends met each other for the first time that day, as he tended to receive them individually. Moreover, he was incredibly choosy; when the famous Madame de Staël visited England, she let him know that she wouldn't call upon anyone until she'd met Bentham. In that case, Bentham replied regretfully, she wouldn't be meeting anybody.

Dissecting the body wasn't the only job Southwood Smith had to do. Bentham had added another important point to his will: the skeleton should be dressed in Bentham's stuffed

Sunday suit and sat on a chair, and the mummified head that had been earlier separated from the body was to be placed on top. Bentham had long prepared for this. He'd made his oven available for mummification experiments, and for the last twenty years of his life he'd carried around with him the glass eyes that were to be inserted into his dried head.

In a posthumous manuscript that wasn't published until 1995, Bentham advocated the widespread uptake of what he had done: leaving one's body to medical science for useful analysis and having one's head turned into an 'auto-icon', a word that Bentham invented himself. Just as an author describes his own life in an autobiography, the auto-icon is 'a man who is his own image'. But what to do with the preserved heads? He mentions the way cannonballs are piled in arsenals, but then rejects this pyramid shape, as it would only allow some of the auto-icons to be on view. Far better, he says, to have them displayed in a wall cabinet or even outside, so long as they were protected from the rain by a layer of copal. In either case, loved ones would be able to visit auto-icons instead of graves. Scholars disagree as to whether or not Bentham was being satirical here.

At any rate, Bentham's last will was faithfully executed. His bones were tied with copper wire and wrapped in straw and a number of other materials, while lavender and naphthalene were used to protect against bugs. At his request, Bentham also kept his walking stick, 'Dapple' (not the only object that Bentham lovingly baptised: we are told that he called his teapot 'Dickey'). Southwood Smith may have been a serious doctor, but he was an amateurish preserver. Bentham's head – dehydrated far too quickly with an air pump and miserably shrunken, with the nose disfigured by sulphuric acid – lost any resemblance to the man himself. Before I show a photograph of it in lectures, I give tender souls the opportunity to cover their eyes (which nobody does, of course).

Soon afterwards, a presentable wax head was put on the body. Bentham's skull, however, served science again seventy-two years after his death. In 1904, the statistician Karl Pearson and his colleague Marie A. Lewenz established comprehensively that there was no truth to the notion that intelligence was linked to head size. They based their study on a substantial volume of data, but Bentham was showcased as a striking example. They made a detailed report about his skull, which turned out to be fairly average in size.

In 1992, Bentham visited Germany. He was part of the exhibition *London: World City, 1800–1840*, under the patronage of Queen Elizabeth II. The other 704 exhibits on view in Essen included the figurehead from HMS *London*; some models of the first steam engines and locomotives; a model of the first calculator, created by Charles Babbage; a mechanical pedometer for horses; and a medal commemorating the end of slavery in the British colonies in 1834.

At that time, Bentham's mummified head still sat between his feet. Then it was kept for a while in a separate box, which was recently opened for a DNA analysis (did he really have

Asperger's? The answer is still inconclusive). A journalist described the smell of the head as a mixture of 'vinegar and feet and bad jerky and dust'.

3

List's Last Economic Triumph

FRIEDRICH LIST
1789–1846

PRESENT
  District medical officer Dr Wieser
  Dr Pfretschner
  Surgeon Engelhart

ASSESSORS
  Josef Walter and Peter Schürle

Once the commission had assembled, the corpse was undressed with the greatest care, laid on the dissecting table, and made ready for the

CORONER'S INQUEST

The corpse is bloated and slightly rigid from the cold, but without being frozen. All the joints of the limbs are stiff; reddish-blue livor mortis is visible on the back, on the sides of the chest, and on the outsides of the arms. The body of the accident victim is five feet four inches, fat, squat, broad-shouldered, and with a short neck. The skull is large, the forehead tall and domed, and as far as can be made out the physiognomy is intelligent and expressive. The irises are light brown, the sparse hair light brown with a little grey, the sideburns are strikingly grey, but the moustache is reddish. In the middle of the crown, where the head is bare, is a triangular wound, the edges projecting outwards. Two sides of this wound are ¾ inch long; the third, pointing forwards, is ½ inch. The fingers of the left hand are desperately clutching the barrel of the pistol, making it difficult to remove.

MEDICAL OPINION

The unusual skull form, the pathological condition of the liver and spleen, the accumulation of solid fat inside the abdominal cavity and thorax, inevitably interrupting circulation, demonstrate that there is a clear disposition to mental illness, namely melancholia.

The final section of this post-mortem report reflects the medical knowledge of 1846, but it also sounds rather unkind about the dead person, even though that is not how it was meant. People who took their own lives, you see, were denied a Christian burial. But, as the Imperial-Royal regional court at Kufstein wrote to the prince-bishop's office, 'It is clear from the post-mortem that the above-mentioned individual suffered so badly from melancholy that free thought and action were impossible, and thus he should not be considered to have committed suicide. It is now requested that the body of this gentleman be buried tomorrow in the usual way.'

And that is what happened. In view of the dead man's fame, all those involved might have felt uneasy at the idea of his being buried outside the cemetery walls. As the regional court had established, the body was 'no doubt [that of] the very well-known German patriot Friedrich List von Augsburg'. The doctor's report and the goodwill of the regional court anticipated the posthumous fame that Friedrich List has undeniably enjoyed: twenty-five schools, one hundred and fourteen streets, and three squares in Germany are named after the man, as well as a street in Reading, Pennsylvania. We shall see why.

Melancholy, the doctors' compassionate diagnosis, is not the only possible reason why List shot himself. And he hadn't led the life of a melancholic – quite the opposite. He was born in 1789, the first year of the French Revolution, as no biographer neglects to mention. When he left his lyceum at the age of fifteen, he had the confidence to reject the simple life path of following his father into the tanner's trade. List's father was a distinguished citizen who had several honorary appointments in the town of Reutlingen and who made it to deputy mayor. With their fine leather, the tanners supplied bookbinders and glove-makers rather than saddlers and shoemakers, and they never used urine for depilation. But they, too, had to thoroughly scrape the stinking remains of flesh and fat from the animal skins in water. Who knows whether or not Friedrich List – had he really wanted to, and had he made a greater effort – could have been more adept in his initial forays into the trade? In any event, at the age of sixteen he began training in a field that properly interested him: public administration.

List learned fast, progressing as quickly as was possible for a 'clerk' on the career path for middle-ranking civil servants. When he was too young to take one of the exams, he passed the time by attending law lectures at the University of Tübingen. He'd seen how the administrative apparatus was hampering the state. Clerks were powerful, and were paid according to the number of pages they wrote – an early example of how supposed performance incentives can backfire, for the officials would substantially pad out proceedings. List advocated reforms and better training for such officials. But not even the university offered everything he thought necessary for these developments. List's efforts led to the establishment of a new faculty of public administration; soon afterwards, he suggested himself as one of the five professors of this faculty – with success. The twenty-eight-year-old offered his profuse thanks to the king of Württemberg for his appointment:

Deeply moved by this great favour, may I be so bold as to offer His Majesty the most humble assurance that my gratitude to His Highest Royal Being is equal to the profound honour which the best Father of the Fatherland has bestowed on me.

May His Majesty deign to accept the sincere assurance that my undertaking to benefit the common good in this post will be no less than my current concern as to whether my feeble vigour will suffice to justify in full His Majesty's trust and to overcome the obstacles that confront every good endeavour.

I am filled with the deepest obeisance

His Royal Majesty's

most humble, faithful and obedient servant

F. List, professor

List's gratitude was genuine – he'd been desperate to become a professor. To achieve this, he was even prepared to earn less than he had as a civil servant. It wasn't easy for the young Professor List in other ways either. He hadn't finished his studies, and did not even have any school qualifications that would have given him the right to study, let alone embark on a PhD. The university's senate, which in effect had no involvement in the appointment, regarded him as a *homo illiteratus*. He'd never addressed an audience before, and he found his public inaugural lecture particularly tough going as it had to be delivered in Latin, a language that List, as a middling student, had no doubt hoped would no longer play a role in his life. The students suspected he was a stooge, unaware that they were speaking of a future political prisoner of the kingdom.

The new professor of public administration saw it as his duty to concern himself not only with administrative reform but with the constitution too. List wasn't contemplating anything revolutionary – only a constitutional monarchy. He trod on the feet, however, of a number of people who soon saw an opportunity to accuse him of dereliction of duty. For List had discovered, in addition to the paralysing state bureaucracy, another economic problem that he was prepared to confront passionately: the customs borders that ran throughout Germany.

At the time, Württemberg had 1.4 million inhabitants. Only three of the thirty-nine states comprising the German Confederation were larger: Bavaria, Prussia, and Austria. The remaining principalities and duchies had populations that each ran into six figures at most; the principality of Hohenzollern-Hechingen was home to a mere 20,000. The relationship between these states was nothing like that between the Länder, or states, of Germany today. When List wanted to wed a woman in neighbouring Baden, he had to ask the king of Württemberg for permission to marry abroad. And then there were the customs that restricted the exchange of goods across the borders of the small states.

Without royal permission, he used the 1819 Easter mass in Frankfurt am Main – i.e. abroad – to establish the German Trade and Industry Association in partnership with some merchants. List was chosen as its head. With powerful eloquence, he formulated the association's petition to the Federal

Assembly. Part of it read, 'To trade between Hamburg and Austria, from Berlin to Switzerland, one must cut across ten states, study ten customs and toll systems, and pay transit duties ten times over. But he who has the misfortune to live on a border where three or four states meet, he spends his entire life amongst hostile customs officials and tariff collectors; that man has no fatherland.'

His activities in the German Trade and Industry Association cost List his professorship; he chose to resign before he could be fired. But he wasn't silenced. As a politician – the voters of Reutlingen had elected him to the Württemberg parliament in 1820 – he saw what burdened the electorate in his hometown. In 1821 he summarised this angrily in a petition:

A world of officials, excluded from the people, scattered across the entire country and concentrated in the ministries, unacquainted with the needs of the people and the conditions of civic life, steeped in endless formalities, claims a monopoly on public administration, combating every citizen's action as if it were subversive, elevating their studies of due form and the advantages of their caste, closely connected by the bonds of kinship, interest, the same education, and the same prejudices. Wherever one looks, one sees nothing but officials, officers, chanceries, assistants, clerks, records offices, jackets for files, official uniforms, prosperity, and luxury from the employees down to the servants.

His tirade continued in the same vein, followed by forty recommendations for reforming the municipal administration. The government was most unhappy that List could use the state parliament as a platform for his manifesto; it worked on the deputies until a majority had List excluded from the chamber. But that wasn't enough – a judge was found who declared that List had infringed the press law, for he'd had the petition reproduced by a printing works and had been denounced by one of the printers, who was hoping for a reward. It was also claimed that the petition insulted officials, judges, and even the king. To atone for all of this, he was to serve ten months' imprisonment. Convicted, List fled Württemberg, but he failed in his attempts to make a life for himself in Strasbourg and Switzerland – or at least to become a professor again.

In 1824, a couple of years after his flight, List returned voluntarily to Württemberg. He hoped in this way to regain the king's favour but was immediately made to serve his sentence in Hohenburg Castle. After five months, he was released early on the condition he relinquish his Württemberg citizenship. This time, he opted for exile overseas, in the US, which had been an independent country for barely fifty years. 'Away! Out of the old rot of 500 years of wickedness and into the New World,' he noted. Without these years in the US, the odd local historian from Württemberg might still know List's name, but no economist would. And yet List began by leading a most unacademic and apolitical life there: he bought a farm and a dozen cows. He didn't last a year as a farmer. One needed a good deal of capital, he complained, to be able to live on agriculture, or one had to be used to hard work. But he was lucky; in August 1826, he took over as editor-in-chief of the *Readinger Adler*, a German-language weekly with 2,500 subscribers.

Soon, however, List no longer found this well-paid job fulfilling. A new canal connecting the Blue Mountains to Reading and Philadelphia stirred his entrepreneurial imagination. He discovered a new coal deposit and was able to buy the land at a good price. But how could the coal be transported to the canal? List and his partner amassed enough capital to build – with the Little Schuylkill Navigation, Railroad and Coal Company – one of the first railway lines in the US.

List's temporary success as a businessman did not prevent him continuing to publish. He wrote about issues of economic policy and planned a textbook called *The American Economist*. This initially came to nothing, but at least he had plenty of material to fall back on when he made a second attempt at a book. He also got involved in American political campaigning, supporting in 1828 the Democratic presidential candidate, Andrew Jackson. The German immigrant vote helped elect Jackson, who would soon have the opportunity to return the favour: after five years in America, List was struck by homesickness, and Jackson was prepared to secure him a post as consul in one of the German states.

List returned to Germany an American citizen and representative, but this didn't stop his old opponents in Württemberg putting a spoke in his wheel. They managed to get the Hamburg senate to reject him as consul. The Saxons, however, were less easily swayed by tales about the dreaded liberal, and eventually List was appointed American consul in the Kingdom of Saxony. He didn't receive a salary for this post, but List had a plan of how he could do something to benefit his German fatherland and at the same time earn money.

As far as the customs borders were concerned, Germany was already heading in the right direction – the German Zollverein (customs union), which came into being in 1834, would make sure of this. But something was still missing, something to bring the states closer together and bolster intra-German trade: good infrastructure.

'Over the course of the past eight years, the state of Pennsylvania has run up debts amounting to no less than 30 million thalers to build canals and railways, and yet it considers itself richer rather than poorer,' List wrote. Thus he beat the drum for railway lines like the one between Dresden and Leipzig, the city he was now living in. That line was opened from 1837 onwards, but his hopes to be offered the post of director foundered; he had to be content with a one-off fee and a gilded silver cup donated by the traders of Leipzig. In 1838, therefore, List moved with his family to Paris, where he earned his money as a journalist, tried to establish a French railway network, and finally found the time to write his magnum opus: *The National System of Political Economy*.

If this book still receives the occasional mention, it is because in it List calls for a protectionist trade policy, one which defends the young domestic industries against superior foreign competition. This makes List popular today in countries like China. But how do his demands square with his old battle against the customs borders that cut through Germany? The answer to this is that List is in favour of free trade between countries that are roughly at the same stage of development; it benefits all of them if they specialise and trade with each other without restrictions. In his typical way, List gives an example of three regions, each producing a single good, the exchange of which shouldn't be impeded by tolls:

> This is arable land, nothing grows there except for wood, whereas in that valley only vines can be planted with any success. Look around your immediate vicinity, my friend, and then answer me this question: can one expect a profit if the people in the arable region agree to snub the wine from the wine region and the wood from the foresters? The natural consequence of this would be that part of the arable area would become woodland and vineyards, while part of the forest and wine regions would be converted into arable, defying nature and to the great detriment of each of the regions.

List's argument, however, is too simplistic in a dynamic world where the list of which goods can be produced in which country is not fixed and unalterable. How can industry develop in an agricultural country if businesspeople are forced to produce only what they do best at the time? Should half of Europe's industrial production be apportioned to Britain forever, as it was in the mid-nineteenth century? According to what List believed, this could only be changed if young industries were protected by tariffs, which today we call 'infant-industry tariffs'. They are not a new idea; they hark back to Alexander Hamilton, the first secretary of the US treasury. Like Germany, America was at the time a country that found it difficult to compete with superior British industry. The US exported products typical of a developing country: cotton and tobacco. In 1791, Hamilton coined the term 'infant industry' for those branches of the economy that were still in need of protection. List expanded this idea with a historical analysis in which he described at length how the successful economic branches of many nations first developed under the protection of tariffs. If those same countries now advocated free trade, according to List, they were denying the less-developed states the path they had successfully taken themselves.

'It is a general maxim', he wrote, 'that, having arrived at the summit of greatness, we throw away the ladder with which we have scaled to the top to take away from others the means to climb after us.' He criticised Britain for having done just that: first protecting and supporting shipping and industry, then calling on other nations, which were in no position to compete, to embrace free trade.

List's infant-industry tariffs were only to last for a limited time, however. Once an industry, protected by customs, has developed, then trade between the US and Britain, for example, has the same advantages as that between Bavaria and Württemberg. But of course it is difficult for politicians to scrap a tariff protecting a certain sector and say, 'Now you're fit for international competition.' The uproar that politicians elicit from associations and lobbyists when they plan to remove a specific tariff is the most important argument advanced by opponents of infant-industry tariffs. Joseph Stiglitz, critic of globalisation and Nobel prize-winner, recommends that infant-industry tariffs shouldn't be introduced to support particular sectors only, but applied uniformly to all industrial goods. Apart from that, he's very much in List's tradition; he expands the list of countries that enjoyed success with infant-industry tariffs with examples from the twentieth century, such as Korea and its steel industry. And Japan, of course: there, in the 1960s, List was popular and industry was protected, whereas now the country has climbed the development ladder and wants to kick it away so others can't clamber up behind. In selecting this example, Stiglitz is clearly paying deliberate homage to List.

The National System of Political Economy brought List a degree of recognition and also some success with sales. During his lifetime a second and third edition appeared, but otherwise he was financially unlucky. He rejected a well-paid permanent position with the French railways because he feared a conflict of loyalties if war broke out between Germany and France. In 1841, he was offered the post of editor of the *Rheinische Zeitung* in Cologne. List was clearly a well-qualified candidate who had founded, published, or been responsible for managing an impressive array of newspapers and periodicals.*

However, shortly before he got the offer from the *Rheinische Zeitung*, List broke a leg and thus didn't feel able to accept it. The historical significance of this rejection was enormous, for then a certain Karl Marx took the job, and soon afterwards Friedrich Engels turned up in the editorial office, offering to send him a few articles from Britain. It was the first meeting between the two men; nobody knows what would have become of Marx without the financial support of his moneyed friend. And what would have become of List?

In November 1846, the month of his death, List was travelling with a passport that authorised him to visit 'at his pleasure the Imperial–Royal Austrian lands, Switzerland, Italy, and Sardinia'. The first section of his journey, from Augsburg to Munich, cost him nothing because on this stretch of railway he had lifelong free travel in recognition of his services. In Kufstein, on the Bavarian–Austrian border, he stayed the night at

---

* Including the *Württembergische Archiv*, the *Volksfreund aus Schwaben*, the *Neckar-Zeitung*, the *Organ für den deutschen Handels- und Fabrikantenstand*, the *Europäische Blätter oder das Interessanteste aus Literatur und Leben für die gebildete Lesewelt*, the *Readinger Adler*, the *National-Magazin für Haus- und Landwirtschaft, National-Unterricht, Statistik und Reisen, neue Erfindungen, National-Unternehmungen und Verbreitung nützlicher Kenntnisse*, the *Eisenbahn-Journal*, and the *Zollvereinsblatt*, for which another title was originally considered, namely *Lists deutsches Centralmagazin zur Förderung sämtlicher materieller Interessen Deutschlands und insbesondere des natürlichen Systems der politischen Ökonomie* ('List's German periodical for the advancement of all of Germany's material interests, especially that of the Natural System of political economy').

the Zum Goldenen Löwen inn, run by Mayor Suppenmoser, who later stated that List had told him Italy was his destination and the purpose of his trip was relaxation.

List was used to taking his life in his hands – and his list of achievements was impressive. He'd become an official rather than an artisan. He'd left the civil service to take up a professorship; kept writing rather than allowing himself to be silenced; progressed in exile from farmer to entrepreneur and found a sympathetic ear in politics in his host country; left the US and returned to Germany; encouraged the construction of the German railways; blocked out the ups and downs of real life at the writer's desk and written a great book on the national economy. What now? Once more, he had to change his life – there was no fortune on which his family could live comfortably – but what to do that was in keeping with the way he'd lived his life till then? Well, there was one thing he could do, and it would enable him to leave behind more than ever before.

List couldn't bring himself to leave a suicide note for his family, but he cleverly made provision for them by writing one to his friend Gustav Kolb. Not that he asked Kolb for anything; he merely proposed a deal, a good deal, by which something infinitely valuable could be gained for the price of something far less valuable. He wrote: 'God have mercy on my relatives… What you and other friends do for those close to me will be rewarded by God. Farewell. F. List.'

As List had hoped, Kolb took the initiative. Newly formed

committees collected 20,000 gulden to support the family, in addition to which King Ludwig I of Bavaria granted List's two single daughters an annuity of 200 gulden, to be paid while they remained unprovided for (that is to say unmarried). The king gave List's widow 400 gulden per year, an income above that of most teachers in Bavaria. Friedrich List's suicide note was his last economic triumph.

4

Thünen and his Gravestone Formula

JOHANN HEINRICH VON THÜNEN
1783–1850

You've succeeded in growing ornamental pumpkins that glow in the dark: a Halloween bestseller. With 1,000 pumpkins you earn €25,000 – €25 a pop! Here's a question: if you want to increase your profit, should you grow more pumpkins?

Your answer will reveal whether you're an economist or not. The right answer is: we don't know. On their own, the figures are not enough to answer the question. What exactly would we need to work this out? How do you calculate how many pumpkins you should grow? The most important contribution to this answer was made by a man who spent most of his life as a farmer in Mecklenburg, in northern Germany. He was one of the last great autodidacts in economics.

Johann Heinrich von Thünen was destined to become a farmer like his father. After going to secondary school in Jever he undertook an agricultural apprenticeship, but he regretted this, considering it a waste of time; he'd wanted to learn far more. He learned Ancient Greek off his own bat, and he acquired his knowledge in agricultural economics at the agricultural colleges founded by the agrarian reformers Albrecht Thaer and Lucas Andreas Staudinger, in Celle and Gross Flottbek, respectively. At the latter, in 1803, not yet twenty years old, he wrote an essay about the local agriculture, in which he very quickly started to digress. He described a country that didn't exist, but which helped him in his deliberations: 'Let us assume that a large city lies in the middle of a country 40 miles in diameter, that this country can only sell its products to the city, and that the agriculture of this district is at the highest level of development. In such a case...' We will see later where this is leading – but, at any rate, here Thünen had put down the first idea for his most important scientific work, *The Isolated State*. He spent his whole life working on this book; the first part appeared in 1826 and the second in 1850, the year of his death. He also remained a farmer all his life.

In 1809, financed partly by his inheritance and partly by credit, he bought Tellow, an estate in Mecklenburg. At 465 hectares, it was slightly bigger than the island of Heligoland. He made use of it for countless studies: does the quality of the wool improve if you feed the sheep differently? What does it cost to lime the soil, and what effect does this have? Can you feed horses with boiled potatoes? What is the increase in the yield of wheat, oats, or potatoes if the topsoil is between two to four inches deeper? He tried out agricultural devices and constructed himself a hook plough. *The Isolated State* is peppered with long passages that use antiquated farming terms. He makes up the costs of his business from his legendary detailed bookkeeping of five laborious years, ranging from the schoolteacher's and nightwatchman's fees and payments to the fire and hail insurance companies to the maintenance of boundary ditches. It's perfectly fine to skip a few dozen pages if you know what you're looking for: the theory of optimal volumes of cultivation (of pumpkins, for example).

Thünen's method is to adjust on paper the amount grown by small increments: 'The ... extra yield always incurs an expenditure of capital and labour, and there must come a point where the value of the extra yield is equal to the extra expenditure.' At that point, the maximum profit has been reached. It doesn't depend, therefore, on the average profit per pumpkin grown so far; the issue is whether *another* pumpkin will cost more than it earns.

What it earns, what the 'value of the extra yield' is, cannot be easily calculated, especially not if you have a patent and are thus the only supplier. By cultivating a few too many pumpkins, you can ruin the price of all your pumpkins. In Thünen's Mecklenburg agriculture, however, another aspect weighed heavier: even if the price per item remains constant, the costs probably won't. For example, if you want to grow more, you might have to do so on poorer soil, which will require more fertiliser.

For his contributions to the theory of production, Thünen is still well known today – amongst specialists in the history

of theory. They know that Thünen was one of the first economists to use differential calculus. Today this is the most
popular mathematic tool amongst economists, for it allows
them to replace notional variation in small increments with
simple calculations. But there is another reason for Thünen's
lasting fame: he is, as the Nobel laureate in Economics Paul
Samuelson called him, the 'founding God' of a completely
new branch of research, 'regional economics'. In all countries,
people – and businesses even more so – have a rather uneven
geographical distribution. What are the reasons for this? What
are the consequences? It's not that nothing comes to mind –
quite the opposite. There are many causes and effects that are
interrelated in all manner of ways. How should we ponder
this? Thünen suggested we begin by envisaging a world where
the problem is clearer:

> Imagine a very large city in the middle of a fertile plain
> without any navigable rivers or canals. The soil is the same
> throughout the plain and uniformly fertile. Far from the
> city, the plain ends in an uncultivated wilderness, cutting
> this state off from the rest of the world.

Thünen's deliberations begin very simply, assuming that there
is only one product that is traded: grain. As his model world is
fictitious, he could also have made up a currency, prices, and
yield volumes, but he takes all the data from his Tellow records.

If you lived close to the market, you could sell 100 kilos of rye for 3.6 thalers. Thünen's estate, however, was 5 Mecklenburg miles (almost 38 km) from the market in Rostock. A cart with four horses travelling for two days would cost him a good 10 per cent of his income, as he would have to pay for repairs and shoeing the horses, while some of the cargo would be eaten by the animals themselves. Because of these transport costs, only 3.1 thalers would be brought back to Tellow rather than 3.6. That figure would be even lower for farms further from the city.

Given this, how should rye be cultivated in Tellow? One option is the simple, labour-saving three-field system of crop rotation, in which one of three fields is left fallow each year and merely ploughed. But you could also switch to the more labour-intensive *Koppelwirtschaft*, another form of rotation, in which fields that are not being used for arable crops in any given year are set to pasture. This increases the yield by 20 per cent, but it is only worthwhile if the outlay for 100 additional kilos of yield is lower than the profit after the deduction of transport costs – in our example, 3.1 thalers; further from the city, the profit would be less, at 2.7 thalers (at 10 Mecklenburg miles, around 75 km) or 1.9 (at 20 miles, around 150 km). If a farm is more than 24.7 miles from the market, Thünen calculates, labour-intensive farming is no longer worthwhile; that is where the three-field system zone begins. The closer we are to the city, the more labour-intensive the cultivation of grain will be; because the trip to the market is shorter, and thus a higher yield gives a greater profit, it is worth extracting more from the soil.

Once we've understood this, Thünen only needs to go one step further: now, in his 'isolated state', it is not only grain that's produced. But the principle remains the same: the more labour required for production, the closer to the market we will find it, and the higher the transport costs for a product, the closer production will be to the city.

The result of this is the famous 'Thünen rings'. In the middle is a city, and around it a first ring with market garden produce such as strawberries and salad – which do not survive a long journey on a cart – and dairy, because in hot weather milk goes off only a few hours after milking. Forestry occupies the second ring, because otherwise its transport would be too expensive. Then comes the particularly labour-intensive crop rotation, *Koppelwirtschaft*, in the fourth ring; the three-field system in the fifth; and extensive livestock farming on the very outside.

Some of this is outdated. For example, it seems quite odd that forestry should be so close to the city, because wood is much easier to transport these days than in Thünen's time. But we still find rings around a city centre; in the middle, things are very labour-intensive, and lots of people provide services there without consuming many materials or taking up much space.

Later, Thünen would attract great admiration for the way he developed his abstract model world of the isolated state – and yet it was in keeping with Thünen's severe short-sightedness that he focused on essentials. From a spa break in Putbus, on the island of Rügen, he wrote:

My short-sightedness is often a hindrance when I am in company. I prefer to make the acquaintance of men who are very tall, very fat, or hunchbacked, as these I am able to recognise. I do not even dare try with women who like chameleons change the colour of what they wear daily.

Focusing on essentials was not just a crutch for Thünen himself; it became so much a life philosophy that he imposed it on others too. When his youngest son, Hermann, undertook a six-month educational trip, he wrote to him in Munich, 'When mentally I put myself in your shoes, I begin to worry about how you will cope with, disentangle, and order such a mass of impressions and ideas.' Whether his son, who was twenty-seven at the time, would ever manage this was something Thünen was not going to leave to chance. Four months later, he picked up his pen and wrote to his half-brother in Oldenburg:

In many respects, I am most pleased that Hermann has been with you for a while now. He has seen such a large number of things and situations that it is impossible for him to process them all and gain overview ... I beg you urgently, dear brother, to show him the way out of the blind alleys of this labyrinth: his happiness depends on it, as does the peace of the days that remain to me.

This sounds more emotive than you'd expect from a northern

German farmer. But the tone was typical of him, and in crises he revealed his true self.

He was sixty-one years old when his wife lay dying. He struggled with despair and sought tranquillity in the fields, which merely served to intensify his pain. As he wrote years later, he cried out, 'The worst criminal can feel no greater agony than that which afflicts me now; wherefore have I deserved this?' He railed against his misfortune, claiming it was unfair, before it occurred to him that the concept of variable natural laws rewarding the good and punishing the wicked is harmful, because it robs each individual of their dignity and the opportunity for selfless virtue. From a hill, he looked down at the village and told himself, 'None of the inhabitants has suffered deprivation; it has not treated any of them unjustly, has not ruined any of them.' He well may have been right; in any event, over the course of the years, Thünen deserved his reputation as a social reformer.

When Thünen bought Tellow in 1809, the estate came with a good one hundred serfs (who he could mortgage or rent out, and who couldn't marry without his permission, but they were allowed to own property, and could even buy their liberty, albeit at a price they'd hardly be able to save up from their meagre wages). In 1820, serfdom was abolished, but this had no effect on poverty. In 1838, Thünen, somewhat horrified, described the cottage of the weaver, not a particularly poor man. It had only two rooms, in which the weaver lived with his wife and four or five children, a journeyman, an apprentice, and a widow. Not to mention the three looms in there.

Thünen built a new house, which the weaver moved into and rented; when the city of Teterow was hit by hunger in 1846, he donated a cartload of rye, followed by two cartloads of potatoes a year later. Politically, he opted for scornful aloofness. His purchase of the estate actually came with a seat in the state parliament, but Thünen wasn't interested; he loathed the backwards Mecklenburg constitution. Although the rulers of the two Mecklenburg duchies had little say over matters of government, the laws were made only by the owners of 'knightly estates' and the representatives of the towns. The separation of powers was an alien concept; the landowners controlled the local police as well as parts of the bureaucracy and judiciary. Large sections of the population had no political representation at all.

Thünen was keen on reform, but not a revolutionary. He would have preferred it if the princes themselves had recognised that the educated middle class were a pillar of the state that ought to be accorded more rights: 'With astonishment and admiration I observed the behaviour of the French people,' he wrote in 1830, when the July Revolution forced the abdication of the reactionary Charles X without leading to anarchy.

He felt very uneasy about the March Revolution of 1848 because of the reports of bloody battles in Berlin. But Thünen didn't fear for his own safety – his workers assured him that nothing would happen to his estate; if necessary, they would defend it themselves. And, ultimately, his optimism triumphed: 'The power of the princes and the arrogance of their omnipotence has now been broken throughout the whole of Germany in a matter of a few weeks.' Now deputies were going to be elected to the National Assembly in Frankfurt – by electors who themselves had been chosen by the local population in constituencies. Thünen was an elector for the district of Belitz, but he was appalled that this role was given to 'two workers in Thürkow, one of them a drunkard; in Warnkenhagen, three workers and a tenant farmer.' He could scarcely believe that in Wattmannshagen 'our Pogge' wasn't elected: 'such a man of honour'.

Thünen thought, therefore, that it was necessary to develop an electoral system based on class, in which some groups of voters could elect more deputies than others. The biggest share should go to the most intelligent: scholars with exam qualifications. The major landowners, too, Thünen believed, ought to elect a greater number of deputies than correlated to their proportion of the population, partly on account of their education, but mainly because their interests were in such close harmony with those of the state.

As far as Thünen was concerned, the lack of workers' education precluded a general and equal franchise, a situation he often lamented and couldn't come to terms with. In vain, he tried to improve school education through the Mecklenburg Patriotic Association; in Tellow, at least, he set up a primary school (for which the pastor trained the tailor to become the teacher). Of course, education doesn't only enable political participation, it also improves the economic lot of the workers. Through education the sons of workers should be able to compete successfully with business owners and thus reduce excessive profit-making. Education has another consequence too: it raises wages almost instantly. This follows from Thünen's theory of market wages:

> The value of the work of the most recently employed worker is also his wage ... The wage, however, that the most recently employed worker receives, must be standardised for all workers of the same skill and competence. For equal performance cannot be remunerated by unequal wages.

Thünen illustrates this point with an example. On an area of 100 square rods, 100 Berlinbushels of potatoes can be grown. One worker can harvest 30 bushels per day – over a tonne in weight, but these are the potatoes that are the easiest to harvest. Additional workers achieve less, because they have to scrape up the earth with the hand hoe to search more thoroughly. Thünen now assumes that four workers harvest 80 bushels daily and that a fifth will give the landowner an additional 6.6 bushels, which can be sold for 33 shillings. If the wage of a worker is less than 33 shillings per day, this fifth worker will be hired; otherwise, he won't. In any event, the last worker to be hired is the one who just manages to earn the landowner as much as he costs.

If the workers are more productive, because they are better trained or because they have better tools, then the business will seek to produce more and will even hire more people to achieve this. If it has to poach these people from other businesses, wages increase. Unfortunately, it can all unravel again. If the workers enjoy a better life, the mortality rate of their children goes down. As a result, there are more workers, and the wage drops back to subsistence level. Now the family earns just enough to survive, and perhaps only if the children help out on the farm as soon as they can rather than going to school.

No, workers who were dependent on the market wage would never be free, and never would they be able to help their children have a better life, Thünen concluded. Estate owners should pay more than the market wage. Thünen embarked on this plan very circumspectly in view of the long-term debts he had, and out of consideration for the landowners around him. In 1836, he gave his most important workers a share in his profits, and in 1848 he extended this to all twenty-one families in the village. From a capital fund, they were paid 4 per cent interest; the capital itself couldn't be called in until they reached the age of sixty, after which it acted as a pension.

Thünen didn't wish to leave the notion of a fair wage to the whim of the landlords. And so, just as he'd found a method to calculate the optimum production volume, he intended to calculate the correct wage. Once again, Thünen used differential calculus, and once again he imagined the example of a simplified model world. At the edge of the isolated state there is more land that everyone can take possession of, but it is not yet cultivated. Before anything can be done with the land, it needs to be cleared, buildings have to be erected, and tools must be manufactured. Thünen assumes that some workers will join forces; most of them will save from their wages everything they don't absolutely need to live and use this to feed the others who cultivate the land and will later work on the estate. By putting their savings into a business, the workers have become capitalists with aspirations to make future profits. What is the wage that achieves the highest possible return on their capital? If it's too low, the workers can't save much, meaning a large number of them will be needed to accumulate the necessary capital and the profits will be shared amongst too many. If the wage is too high, then the costs of the new estate are too high. The highest possible wage, at which no profit accrues, Thünen calls p, and the subsistence wage that merely secures the minimum existence he calls a. Thünen then calculates the wage A, at which the 'worker capitalists' maximise their capital return: $A = \sqrt{a * p}$.

If the subsistence wage is 3 and the highest possible wage 12, then the product of these is 36, and the square root of this, 6, is the 'natural wage', as Thünen calls it. Scholars still argue about how flawless his mathematical derivation actually is, but any improvements in Thünen's method don't change the result. Even so, economists regard the formula as irrelevant; it only holds true in Thünen's quirky model world, and only if its inhabitants merely wish to maximise their return (rather than what they earn overall, including their wage). And, ultimately, there's only one scenario in which it's certain that Thünen's 'natural wage' would improve the workers' situation: if they had been getting the subsistence wage beforehand. Otherwise the market wage could even be higher than Thünen's fair wage.

At all events, the fair wage was the core of the second volume of *The Isolated State*, which came out in 1850, the year in which Thünen died of a stroke. He'd been working on the book for a long time, having penned one of the chapters back in 1826, when the first volume had just been published. In 1843, he wrote, 'Ever since I can remember I have been impelled to carry out this study by a truly mysterious power ... I must be able to use this in another world, for I do not know what pulls me to it with such force.' He was almost sixty years of age, and his health had never been particularly robust. He would have found it difficult to banish thoughts about the time after death.

What was to go on his gravestone? Nobody would have been surprised if Thünen had asked for 'his' rings. They are decorative, and they cemented his fame (posthumously too – the rollable school-wall maps they made their way on to are out of fashion now, but Thünen's rings can still be found in agricultural economics textbooks and are in every primer on regional economics). But no, he chose his formula for the fair wage. The gravestone still exists in the village church cemetery at Belitz, near Tellow. The locals are used to bumping into economists who make the pilgrimage to Thünen's grave and find it most uplifting that the engraving $A = \sqrt{a * p}$ honours the quest rather than the achievement.

5

Chayanov: Death in Hell

ALEXANDER V. CHAYANOV
1888–1937

It may come as a surprise that in 1920, in the three-year-old Soviet Union, a novel appeared that pulled the Soviet economic system to pieces. The book suggests that socialism only came about because the tormented, apathetic workers couldn't conceive of any other objective to their struggle than more factory work – only this time not in a capitalist torture chamber – and that socialism then became another system unfit for purpose, having too many underlings and too little opportunity for creativity.

Even so, the book was published. The path from the 1917 October Revolution to the terror of the Stalinist dictatorship wasn't a straight one. In the early years of the Soviet Republic, cultural life was lively and colourful. An astonishing number of non-socialist plays were performed in theatres, and publishing houses were still printing all manner of works, including the aforementioned novel *The Journey of*

My Brother Alexei to the Land of Peasant Utopia by Alexander V. Chayanov.

Chayanov, born in 1888, had been professor at a Moscow institute of agricultural economics since 1913, and since 1919 he'd also been working in the Russian Soviet Republic's ministry of agriculture, although ministries were then called People's Commissariats. But he wasn't a dilettante who did a bit of writing in his spare time. *The Journey* wasn't his first literary publication, and it's possible that fans of Russian fantastic fiction who still read his tale *The Venetian Mirror* outnumber the readers of his academic works.

Chayanov used his literary talent to bring his economic ideas to a wider audience. The hero of *The Journey* is one Alexei Kremnev, a trained lawyer and socialist functionary. It's 1921 and he's running a department in the 'Global Economic Council', but in a rather bourgeois way he's not especially satisfied with the results of the revolution. Alone in the library of his terribly middle-class apartment, he has silent conversations with progressive, non-socialist authors, whom he accuses of having nothing better to offer than socialism, which – admittedly – is still incomplete. Then things get creepy: there is a whiff of sulphur, a book by Alexander Herzen shuts by itself, the hands of the clock whizz around ever more quickly, the sheets of the tear-off calendar come loose and fly around the room… It's dark; Kremnev bumps into unfamiliar objects and, when he finally drops onto a sofa that wasn't there before, he passes out.

He wakes up in a strange world. The furniture is red with yellow-green covers. Looking out of the window, he knows he's in Moscow because he can see the Kremlin, but all the monumental architecture is gone, including the tallest building from the pre-revolutionary era – all ten stories of it. Instead, there are… gardens! 'Have I become the hero of a utopian novel?' Kremnev exclaims (a rather unsubtle aid the author provides for the slow-witted amongst his readers). Then he finds a paper and notes the date: 5 September 1984.

It turns out that Kremnev has woken up in an apartment belonging to the Minin family, who think he's a visitor from America called Charlie Man, even though they're surprised by his fluent Russian – with a Moscow accent too – and also by the fact that modern American fashion is remarkably similar to that from old Minin's childhood. Also in the family are two attractive and kind sisters, Katarina and Paraskeva, named not entirely coincidentally after the Slavic goddesses of mothers and agriculture, as well as their brother Nikifor, who explains Russian society in 1984 to the supposed American visitor.

One of Chayanov's flights of fancy may have excited the Bolsheviks. In 1984, the people control the weather with the help of 'meteorophors', but how they work remains a mystery to Kremnev. Rain is no longer forecast; it's scheduled for such-and-such a time.

This apart, though, the novel offers up one affront after another. Since 1934, we learn, power has been firmly in the hands of the peasant parties. (These parties are only mentioned once; Chayanov could have left them out, and years later will have cursed himself for not having done so.) In 1944 came the order to destroy the cities in Chayanov's utopia. In the wake of this, only 100,000 inhabitants remain in Moscow, and in fact there are no longer cities as we know them, merely places where people gather for festivities and assemblies and where they go to school, the library, or the theatre. Every peasant can get to the nearest town in ninety minutes at the most, flying in 'aeropils' if necessary. Most people are peasants who farm their own small parcels of land, a healthy and creative activity for which family farms prove ideal, because the high population density means that 'almost every ear of corn has to be cared for individually'. Such work cannot be mechanised.

So, in this utopia, do large businesses have any remaining advantages over small ones? Yes, in manufacturing they do, which is why no family firms exist in that sector any longer. Most businesses are cooperatives ('collectively managed businesses'), which are superior to state firms in which mainly managers prosper.

Competition plays an important role in this world. Performance-based pay has been introduced, and it keeps a few classical capitalist businesses afloat – the best ones. The organisational and technical genius of some capitalists allows them to pay the high taxes they are burdened with. As big fishes in a small pond, these firms prevent the cooperatives from slacking.

After the global revolution, moreover, the spread of socialism across the planet has been merely temporary. A six-month war saw the world split into five economic systems. Anglo-France became capitalist again under a Soviet oligarchy; America reintroduced parliamentarism and, in part, private ownership of the means of production; Sino-Japan returned to a monarchical system; Russia is now run by the peasantry; and only Germany is still conventionally Soviet. All other parts of the world are colonies, divided pretty much evenly between the five systems.

Over time, Kremnev's situation becomes critical, not least because people are surprised at how poorly 'Charlie Man' speaks English. With Germany trying to provoke a war, he is imprisoned as a German spy. The war breaks out, but it is thankfully short: a wall of wind stops the German army in its tracks, and meteorophors destroy the German aircraft. Berlin surrenders. Reparations take the form of paintings (Botticelli, Holbein, etc.) for the travelling exhibitions that delight the art-loving Russian peasants, as well as the Pergamon Altar and thousands of stud bulls of a breed for which the cruel spirit that guides history supplied the author with a brilliant name: 'Only-for-Germany'.

The novel ends with Kremnev's release from prison, facing an uncertain future. As the entire work is referred to as 'Part I', Chayanov must have planned a sequel we know nothing about. For us readers, his story will forever finish with a kiss that Katharina plants on Kremnev's forehead. Despite the ending, there is no reason to pity Kremnev, when we compare his fate to Chayanov's. The prison Kremnev is taken to is the concert hall of a hotel that has been kitted out with camp beds. The commandant apologises for the conditions but says that it might only be for a couple of days, and that the authorities will try to make up for it with good food and entertainment. The interrogation, in which Kremnev attempts to make his story sound plausible, is more like a hearing by a respectable committee of experts. Poor Chayanov would undergo a quite different experience.

In 1921, the year after the publication of Chayanov's novel, agriculture in the Soviet Union was booming. The cooperatives through which independent small farmers obtained tools and fertiliser and could sell their produce were nationalised. Chayanov, a passionate advocate of cooperatives, was incensed: 'It's not possible for the state to press the ox into the form of a camel and insist he stays alive.'

Moreover, the peasants had to hand over so much grain that it often left them without seed. The spring of 1921 saw the start of the great famine that would end up costing five million lives. The resentment of the workers over such scant provision threatened the Bolsheviks' power. Lenin agreed to the setting up of an aid committee consisting of around eight people, including a few prominent non-communists, and Chayanov. They used their reputations and their connections abroad to appeal for assistance, not without success. The International Red Cross helped out, as did the American Relief Administration, which was run by future US president Herbert Hoover.

Once the assistance was up and running, Lenin was keen to get rid of the committee members; they'd seen too clearly how the government had failed, and they'd articulated this too. Most were exiled, but two were given death sentences, which were overturned following international protest. Even Lenin's old comrade Maxim Gorky was advised in no uncertain terms to take a 'holiday' abroad; the writer had served as the committee's spokesman. Chayanov, highly regarded by Lenin and promoted to director of the economics institute shortly beforehand, received a similarly mild reprimand: he was sent on a long work trip.

He made use of the time. Barely had he arrived in Britain in May 1922 than he threw himself into work on the book that would make him famous. Other stops on his trip were Schreiberhau in Silesia (now in Poland), and Heidelberg. At the time, around 700,000 Russian emigrants lived in Germany. Chayanov spoke passably good German, but he wrote in Russian and used a translator for the German edition of the book that appeared in the summer of 1923: *The Theory of Peasant Economy*.

Chayanov saw a major contradiction between capitalist businesses and family farms. The former seeks to maximise profit, whereas peasants who are fit enough to work do so as much as they have to – which means as long as they need to in order to feed their families. Once this objective has been achieved, Chayanov says, 'no wage, no matter how high, can tempt the peasant to work'. On the other hand, it's possible that such a family puts far more work into its farm than a capitalist business with employees would. If the revenue for one work hour is below the hourly wage, the capitalist firm keeps letting employees go until this is no longer the case. Unprofitable labour-intensive activities cease. This is unlike in the family farm, where people will if necessary overwork themselves to feed the family – in this case, labour-intensive products are grown to extract from the soil whatever can be got out, even though the revenue per work hour is very low.

Like Chayanov's novel, his analysis is provocative. The Bolsheviks would have noticed this even if Chayanov hadn't written that the Marxist system 'provided completely inadequate tools'. Orthodox Marxism expected an increasing concentration into fewer and thus larger businesses in agriculture too; every farmer could be a budding capitalist – an opponent of revolution and progress. Now Chayanov came along and claimed that the justification for expropriation and collectivisation was worthless.

All the same, Chayanov decided to return to Russia in the autumn of 1923, for several reasons. First there was 'his' agricultural institute, where thirty academics worked and which was equipped with a large library of around 100,000 volumes. No doubt the ability to access detailed statistics on Russian agriculture was also enticing.

He hoped to be able to help, and indeed it looked as if economic reason were returning to Russia. Lenin had ended 'war communism', meaning, amongst other things, that harvests were no longer pointlessly confiscated, and the state gave up organising trade in food completely by itself. It was an accomplishment of Chayanov and some of Lenin's other economic advisers that the peasants only had to surrender a certain share of their harvests for the 'New Economic Policy'. When the 'natural tax' was paid, the peasants could keep the rest for themselves and make use of it. So there were still incentives for making an effort when farming the land.

Another motive for Chayanov's return may have been his love for his home city of Moscow. The daughter of one of his colleagues recalled walks Chayanov sometimes invited her to join him on, during which he revealed himself to be a knowledgeable and outgoing city guide. Apart from this, we know little about his personality, for his diaries and letters were confiscated and destroyed. In most of the photographs that have survived of Chayanov, he's looking not at the camera but slightly to the left, from the photographer's perspective, gazing somewhat melancholically into the distance, lost in thought.

To begin with, he was left to work undisturbed, and in 1925 *The Theory of Peasant Economy* appeared in Russian. The English translation of 1966 heralded a Chayanov renaissance, and the German edition was reprinted several times. But why? Nothing remains of many economic analyses after a century apart from a pile a dust. Chayanov's work, by contrast, has remained remarkably fresh. Nowadays we take for granted that economic decisions are not just driven by monetary considerations, but by psychological factors too. In a modern way,

Chayanov explains why farmers sometimes make more effort and sometimes less: it is a 'peculiar balance between the satisfaction of one's needs and the arduousness (degree of toil) of the work'. Economists today would merely delete the word 'peculiar'; Chayanov-like analyses now belong to the academic mainstream.

Chayanov's book is stuffed with statistics and statistical evaluations; here, too, he was a modern economist. (We learn, for example, that men in Russia's Tver district worked only 2,206 of the 5,876 available waking hours in a year, meaning they could have put in far more labour had this been necessary to sustain their families.) Some of what he wrote was only applicable to the world in which he lived. In developed Western countries, it's certainly no longer the case that farmers have no interest in surpluses and that they work just enough to satisfy the basic needs of the family (although Chayanov does concede that what constitutes a basic need can differ from period to period and from place to place). And what about Chayanov's conclusion that family farms, with 'extraordinary tenacity and resilience', survive crises that close down capitalist businesses and are thus the natural practitioners of agriculture?

At first glance, you might argue that today's 'industrial' agriculture has little in common with that in Chayanov's Russia. Modern combine harvesters look as if an unimaginative child has built a battle robot with outsized Lego. Drivers climb into these machines via tall ladders and work fields that you'd think could accommodate an airport or even two. But this impression is deceptive. Farms are not so monstrously big; for example, only 0.5 per cent of farms in Germany today can boast more than the 1,000 hectares that airports such as Cologne Bonn, Boston, or Beijing make do with. And farms are mainly run by families. Five out of every seven people who work on family farms in Germany are members of that family.

So Chayanov was right: family farms do not disappear by themselves. The political power of the peasants, however, remained limited to Chayanov's fictional novel world. Ten years after the October Revolution, and five after the publication of *The Theory of Peasant Economy*, a new wave of collectivisation took place. And a bad time began for the ideology-free pursuit of knowledge.

The first blow was manageable. The Research Institute of Agricultural Economics and Agricultural Policy was closed down in 1928. Chayanov lost his post of director but remained a professor at the university. But then came 27 December 1929. Stalin, who'd become Lenin's successor in 1924, gave a speech at a conference of Marxist agricultural economists that reads like a tirade against Chayanov, even though his name only occurs once: 'It is … incomprehensible why the anti-scientific theories of Soviet economists of the Chayanov mould should continue to be disseminated unchecked in our press.'

This wasn't just criticism – it was a sentence. On 21 June 1930, Chayanov was arrested at his workplace and interrogated at Lubyanka, the central prison building of the Soviet secret service. Lubyanka saw many forced confessions, leading to convictions for counter-revolutionary activity or membership of terrorist associations. Sometimes even more absurd charges were concocted, such as 'conspiracy to destroy the fatherland with secretly constructed artificial volcanos'. Chayanov admitted to setting up a 'fighting organ for the rump bourgeoisie', namely the 'Active Peasants Party'. It's possible that the secret service was inspired by Chayanov's novel; he'd never belonged to a political party, and the Active Peasants Party didn't exist. Under interrogation, Chayanov spun out endless details about the party. We read, for example, of young members who are prepared 'to resort to terrorist-like measures' that Chayanov himself opposed. There were also far-right currents in the party, he said, of which 'the agricultural economists from the periphery' were the most reactionary. The protocol states that Chayanov's institute was working for the party, for example by publishing books in which their petit-bourgeois ideology reached an international audience. Chayanov's 1923 book was one of these. Moreover, the institute was said to have 'connections to more than fifty foreign academic-ideological centres'.

Chayanov was also forced to talk about people, in particular other agricultural economists at the institute. Some he associated with the Active Peasants Party, others he protected as best he could. For example, he said that his colleague Alexander Minin had planned a work trip to Germany, Denmark, and Czechoslovakia. He'd given Minin, who was supposed to make contact with certain academics, some letters of recommendation: 'All these requests by me must be seen as part of my work with the party's contacts abroad, which I've described in detail in a separate statement. I did not get the impression, however, that our conversation had the character of a political briefing.'

It is no coincidence that one of the characters in *The Journey of My Brother Alexei to the Land of Peasant Utopia* is also called Minin; Chayanov often named characters in his stories after real people. One, for example, was named after Mikhail Bulgakov, who later became famous as the author of *The Master and Margarita*. Towards the end of Chayanov's novel, it's Minin who does his civic duty and denounces the first-person narrator, Kremnev.

Chayanov put on record what had to be put on record. Otherwise, he put up a fight. He said he'd realised his academic errors two years earlier; what he was writing now showed the high opinion he had of large agricultural enterprises. He was keen to make an active contribution to the success of Soviet policy, he insisted, and his more recent works could be used for propaganda abroad. In a letter to a secret intelligence officer, he wrote:

I beg my life be spared, and I swear to devote the rest of it to socialist agriculture, to which objectively I have already made a not-insignificant contribution ... If at the front you seize a twelve-inch cannon from the enemy, you don't destroy it, but turn it against the enemy.

I am one of the best scientists in the world in my field and there is much I can do for you. Treat me as you would a cannon captured from the enemy. I will do all I can for socialism.

He asked to have his confiscated books returned, and requested a pillow. Because of his frail health, he had to lie down for long periods, and his head was numb. Despite this, he wrote a manuscript about socialist irrigation farming and wrote letters in which he suggested ideas for research projects.

The interrogations lasted for a year after his arrest. He was released from prison in 1934 and exiled to Alma-Ata in Kazakhstan, where he worked for a while in the republic commissariat for agriculture. On 17 March 1937, he was re-arrested, interrogated over and over again, and, on 3 October 1937, three months before his fiftieth birthday, sentenced to death by firing squad by the military council of the Supreme Court of the Soviet Union.

The execution was carried out immediately. It was one of 700,000 shootings during the Great Terror of 1937–8. The victims also included Alexander Minin and the secret service officer who'd interrogated Chayanov in 1930.

6

Keynes: An Economist, Amongst Other Things

JOHN MAYNARD KEYNES
1883–1946

'He was one of the most intelligent and most original thinkers I have known, but economics was just a sideline for him.' You wouldn't think it possible that this double-edged praise could be referring to the most famous economist of the twentieth century, John Maynard Keynes. The quotation is from Friedrich von Hayek, a friend and academic adversary of Keynes. According to Hayek, Keynes knew little about the economy of the nineteenth century, because his interests were driven by aesthetic considerations and he happened to hate the nineteenth century. He was barely familiar with the academic literature of that time, whereas he was a great expert on the Elizabethan age. But, sure, Keynes would have had what it takes to be a great economist if only he'd focused on it.

Although Keynes's collected works comprise thirty volumes, Hayek was not completely wrong. Keynes devoted much attention, time, and money to the arts. He was one of the

Bloomsbury Set – the famous group of artists and intellectuals that included Virginia Woolf, E. M. Forster, Lytton Strachey, and Roger Fry. He owned works by Cézanne, Delacroix, and Ingres. The last book he read before he died was the first edition of a volume by the Irish poet Thomas Parnell.

Keynes hadn't inherited the fortune that allowed him to collect art; he'd earned it through speculation. But there were also years of losses – he was well aware that securities didn't offer risk-free profit and that the financial markets were almost impossible to figure out, even irrational. In his key work, *The General Theory of Employment, Interest and Money*, he demonstrates this with a neat thought experiment.

Imagine you're taking part in a newspaper competition, in which you have to choose the six most beautiful portrait photographs out of a hundred. You can win if your choice best matches the average choices of the other participants. (If this strange rule seems familiar, it's because it's the basis of the television game show *Family Fortunes*.) Which photos do you choose? Do you really plump for the ones you think are the most beautiful? The trouble is, you don't think your taste corresponds to the average. So you wonder: which six photographs do the other participants like best? But hang on a second. You know they're thinking the same thing. So you have to guess which are the six photographs that the others believe most other people think... And you quickly realise that such deliberations will never lead to a sensible conclusion.

The same problem, according to Keynes, is faced by

investors who wonder if they should buy a particular share, for example. If other investors think it's a good idea to buy the share, the value will rise. What do the other investors base their decision on? Whether they believe the others think the value of the share will rise. But whether the others believe this depends on whether they think the others think that the others think… It's impossible to predict when a stock market bubble will burst.

Nonetheless, Keynes also invested money for his Bloomsbury Set friends. He shouldn't have expected much gratitude for this, as at times he was regarded as a sort of accountant – economists don't exactly take this as a compliment, but sometimes a bit of economic bookkeeping gets them a long way. This can be seen by the banana parable that Keynes devised.

Imagine a country where the economy works very simply: the only product that's needed and produced is bananas. The money that the inhabitants of this country don't spend on bananas they save. The banks lend that money to entrepreneurs, who use it to maintain or expand the banana plantations. Now, the country's finance minister comes up with the idea of calling on its citizens to be especially thrifty. If the campaign is successful, people will bring more money to the bank and spend less on bananas. Does this mean the entrepreneurs will invest more? Not necessarily, for it depends on the yields they're expecting, which in turn depends on what the others are expecting… You know the story. The frugality campaign could also have an impact on the entrepreneurs themselves, or in the short term there might be insufficient manpower to expand the plantations, or... Keynes's list of reasons why the entrepreneurs have no desire to invest at that point is fairly long. And, of course, now that the consumers are more thrifty, they're unwilling to spend as much as before. So what happens to banana production? Keynes thought out his example of bananas particularly well; had it been nuts, the growers could have stored them and tried to sell them later. But bananas must get to the consumers immediately. So what choice do the entrepreneurs have but to lower the prices? The result seems fanciful. The price of bananas falls so low that, as before, people can buy the entire harvest, but now they've also got savings in the bank. Has the finance minister worked a miracle? Have they all become richer?

The banana parable from 1930 is a small step on the path towards Keynes's completely new view of economic relations. Maybe it helped him that he hardly knew many works by economists who were older than his own teacher, Alfred Marshall. Thomas Parnell wrote, in probably the last poem that Keynes read before his death, 'A Night-Piece on Death':

Their books from wisdom widely stray,
Or point at best the longest way.
I'll seek a readier path, and go
Where wisdom's surely taught below.

The 'readier path' that Keynes goes down is his own model

world. In it, we're now looking at the banana plantations. If prices fall but wages remain constant, profits will sink and soon become losses. If prior to the frugality campaign the entrepreneurs have made neither a profit nor a loss, then now their losses are as high as the sum of new savings. The country hasn't become richer – we can only believe it has if we allow ourselves to be deceived by irrelevant bank balances. The best thing here is to think as simply as possible: if there are no more bananas, the country can't be richer.

Unfortunately, the story doesn't end there. The losses force the entrepreneurs to either lower wages or let people go. But that doesn't help them, for afterwards the consumers can't buy as many bananas – which means the entrepreneurs make even more losses, wages sink again or more people are let go, and so fewer bananas are planted and harvested. Now, before everyone starves, the finance minister will turn the frugality campaign into a consumption campaign, or the state will compensate for the drop in demand for bananas with its own investments.

Is Keynes always so easy to understand? Not at all. Between the banana parable and his *General Theory* lie six years of work, which focused on his new theoretical construct rather than the way he described it. Paul Samuelson is blunt in his assessment:

It is a badly written book, poorly organized; any layman who, beguiled by the author's previous reputation, bought the book was cheated of his 5 shillings ... Flashes of insight and intuition intersperse tedious algebra. An awkward definition suddenly gives way to an unforgettable cadenza. When it finally is mastered, we find its analysis to be obvious and at the same time new. In short, it is a work of genius.

Many economists steer clear of Keynes's book. The fact that he is so popular and that there is a theory known as Keynesianism – or, actually, three or four of them – is down to his interpreters, although they're not always in agreement on the meaning. The exceptions are those elements of Keynes's theory that he explained very clearly. He certainly held the views that the behaviour of investors is unpredictable, that there is no economic calculation that can be described by a single mathematical equation, and that economies can be thrown into turmoil and require bold state intervention.

Is this really so terribly important? Isn't material life ultimately insignificant in comparison to intellectual pleasures? What remains of wealth in the end? The place where Thomas Parnell seeks the truth, which he no longer expects to get from books, is the cemetery. One last time (although it doesn't help the dead person), Parnell wrote, there are economic differences here:

Those graves, with bending osier bound,
That nameless heave the crumpled ground,
Quick to the glancing thought disclose
Where Toil and Poverty repose.

At least names are chiselled into flat gravestones, but before long – even before they become illegible – nobody will remember them.

> A middle race of mortals own,
> Men, half ambitious, all unknown.

And then there are the marble tombs with coats of arms and angels, shining in the light of the moon. In this spooky atmosphere, death addresses the poet and, in a surprising turn, speaks words of comfort.

The last surviving comment Keynes made before his death was a take on this poem. Don't worry, he interpreted it as saying, divine justice comes in the end. Or, in the words of Parnell, with death the 'chains are cast aside', and the pious soul spreads its wings and flies away.

That sentiment doesn't sound much like Keynes, though. Yes, he died at the age of sixty-two from a heart attack, having survived an earlier one, but he couldn't know that Parnell's book would be the last one he'd hold in his hands. His comments on *A Night-Piece on Death* were not meant to be a legacy, and his famous dictum, 'In the long run we are all dead', wasn't a consolation but a trenchant warning that short-term disruptions are worth thinking about.

Keynes didn't live as if he were saving anything for after death. He associated with important intellectuals, becoming particularly close to a number of them. His lovers included

– besides other male members of the Bloomsbury Set – Lytton Strachey, one of the most waspish writers of the twentieth century. But then Keynes baffled his friends by marrying the Russian star ballerina Lydia Lopokova. He worked in various roles for the British government and advised politicians, who had to put up with a lot from him. Apparently, when Keynes arrived with Prime Minister Herbert Henry Asquith at a function near Oxford, a butler announced them as 'Mr Keynes and another gentleman'. And, in 1928, Keynes wrote to Winston Churchill, 'Dear Chancellor of the Exchequer, what an imbecile Currency Bill you have introduced!' Churchill replied very politely and respectfully, beginning, 'My dear Keynes'. After 1942, he could have written 'Lord Keynes', for the economist had been made a peer.

Did Keynes miss out on anything? Yes, he said shortly before his death in 1946: he ought to have drunk more champagne. If we wish to find a poem that better suits Keynes than the cemetery verse of Parnell the theologian, then perhaps these lines from the German poet Uwe Gressmann, who died young, are appropriate:

He who at the end of the road
Still mourns the drink
But has to enter the dark house
Has only half emptied the green cup

7

Stackelberg: The Other Führer

HEINRICH FREIHERR VON STACKELBERG

1905–1946

Businesspeople fret about their costs and prices. On many markets, it's a smart move to come up with the right course of action by observing the behaviour of other providers. Particularly shrewd, however, are those entrepreneurs who tell themselves, 'The others are watching what I do; I know they're doing this; can I use this knowledge?' Heinrich Freiherr von Stackelberg was the first economist who developed a practicable theory about such businesspeople. Every student in a beginner's lecture about markets and prices learns the Stackelberg leadership model; many students in Germany, where it is known as 'Stackelberg-Führer', have to put up with their lecturers joking that Stackelberg was quite a Nazi. A cheap joke, yes, but it's not unduly harsh on the man.

Stackelberg was twenty-six and had spent time in various junior Nazi associations when, in 1932, he became editor of *Jungnationale Stimmen*, trumpeting such phrases as 'A biological consideration of the *Volk* raises first and foremost the issue of race. In the blood of all of us is the desire to preserve the purity of the breed.' The publication also addressed issues raised by people who were more level-headed, for example: 'the scientist and the National Socialist – how are the two compatible?' Stackelberg answered this question in 1934 as 'head of lecturers at the University of Cologne':

> The researcher is free to go the way his conscience guides him. But not everyone may become a researcher. In personality and character, he must be worthy of research in the name of the nation. The researcher must be a National Socialist ... by acknowledging the nation in all its estates and classes as the highest worldly asset, and pledging unconditional allegiance to its leader, Adolf Hitler.

Such researchers, he wrote, could be left to their own devices, allowing 'National Socialist, German science to develop'. Two years earlier, Stackelberg had demonstrated what this would look like when he turned emphatically against free trade, because the international division of labour made the nation dependent on foreign production, which, he argued bluntly, was fatal, especially in wartime. Elsewhere, he employed circumlocution in phrases such as 'liberation of those sections of the German people outside of the Reich'.

At the time, German economics as a discipline had been pursuing its own agenda for a number of years without producing much of note. Strangely, Stackelberg was one of the pioneers who picked up on important international research such as that by the British socialist Joan Robinson. An academic ancestor of the two was the French mathematician Antoine-Augustin Cournot, who had contemplated how a (fictional) entrepreneur with a monopoly on a certain healing water works out its price. This is a clever example for two reasons. First, healing water can't be substituted by any other water; the entrepreneur needn't worry about competition. Second, the water costs them next to nothing. Yes, they may have to do a bit of advertising and purchase a bottling plant, but 1,001 bottles aren't going to cost any more than 1,000. Very practical: first analyse a problem, then keep it as simple as possible.

In Cournot's honour, let's call this monopolist Antoine. How many bottles should Antoine sell? As many as possible? That doesn't make any sense, as he'd only find additional buyers if he lowered the price. He'd attract most buyers if he reduced the price to zero, but then the revenue would be zero too. The price mustn't be too high either, because although that would give a fantastic profit per bottle, he might only sell one. Somewhere in-between these two extremes lies the optimal volume, and thanks to Cournot we've been able to work out exactly where.

The demand for healing water is not merely dependent on the price; other factors come into play too. Perhaps the place where the source originates becomes better connected via a new railway line. Delighted by this, Antoine does his Cournot calculations, and the result is a higher price, higher volumes, and a higher profit. If this is mitigated by an unexpectedly chilly summer, meaning that fewer tourists visit the source area, our Antoine will sell less. And now we're going to allow something quite disagreeable to happen: a second source is discovered that spouts healing water with exactly the same properties. For the Cournot ex-monopolist Antoine, the effect is similar to bad weather. Because there is now a competitor who sells 500 bottles, the demand for his own bottles is less. He must recalculate the volume he should produce and the price to sell it at. His competitor – let's call him Bernard – proceeds to do the same. Now Bernard produces more than before. Antoine does his sums again. He fills fewer bottles; Bernard fills a few more. At some point, this process ends when we've reached an equilibrium.

Stackelberg didn't find Cournot's solution convincing. The weather and the competition are both important for Antoine, but there is a major difference. Let's consider the weather first. Antoine has taken his umbrella out with him for the past ten days but never needed to use it. Now, on the eleventh day, he forgets his brolly and it promptly begins to rain. You might think there's someone up there in heaven just waiting to soak us. It's a funny thought, but nobody really believes it's true. On sober reflection, the weather doesn't give a fig about Antoine.

Unlike the weather god, Bernard does take a close look at what Antoine's up to. If Antoine produces less, Bernard will fill more bottles. Why can't Antoine just predict this? After all, chess players don't regard their opponents' moves as a natural phenomenon. Every chess player knows that their opponent is searching for the best move. Stackelberg showed that, employing such foresight, a business sharing the market with a competitor can also profit. The business that looks ahead produces more and reaps a greater profit than one which only ever reacts.

But what if Antoine *and* Bernard adopt the position of forward-looking business? If both act on the assumption that their rival adjusts to their own decision-making, whereas in fact neither reacts, then the result is chaos. This muddle, to Stackelberg's mind, is best resolved by the intervention of the fascist state.

And yet, his SS comrades took exception to his having a church wedding in 1936, while soon afterwards Heinrich Himmler wound up the Baltic Brotherhood, a sort of elite order that Stackelberg belonged to. The fact that Stackelberg didn't get on equally well with all Nazis has been presented in his favour by sympathetic biographers. But his leaving Germany in 1943 wasn't of much use to those defending his reputation, because he went to Madrid, the capital of a country facing another thirty years of dictatorship under General Franco. Stackelberg fitted perfectly into the country in other ways, since he'd learned Spanish as a child from his Argentinian mother. Physically, too, his mother's influence triumphed over his father's genes from a knightly Baltic family: Stackelberg was a handsome man with dark eyes. If he'd combed his hair back rather than sticking with a severe military parting, he could have been mistaken for a tango singer.

In 1951, he could have been appointed professor of economic theory at the University of Bonn, where he could have become dean of the faculty of law and economics in 1960. In 1970, potentially the year of his retirement, he could have been awarded the Order of Merit of the Federal Republic of Germany and spent two more years as chair of the academic advisory board to the ministry of economics. In 1946, however, Heinrich von Stackelberg died of lymph node cancer in Madrid.

8

Schumpeter Prays to the Rabbits

JOSEPH ALOIS SCHUMPETER
1883–1950

Joseph Alois Schumpeter was a touch overweight. He had rubbery lips, thick, strangely rounded eyebrows and a watery gaze. His ears stuck out slightly. Otherwise there was nothing striking about his face, and he didn't have enough hair to make up for this deficit with a snappy hairstyle.

Yet nobody who'd been familiar with Schumpeter's face would describe him like this, even though every detail is accurate. So let's try again. Joseph Alois Schumpeter had eyebrows which, through a whim of nature, made him look as if he were raising them. While Schumpeter's full lips seemed to signal an overpowering sensuality, his practically bald head aroused tender and totally innocent feelings in many women. In Schumpeter's life and death women played a major role, though he wasn't always a ladykiller. He didn't die in a duel either.

There's not much out of the ordinary about the first half of his life; everything resembled a smooth academic career in the Habsburg Monarchy. This he owed to his mother. To give her Joseph the chance of a good education after his father died when the boy was four, she moved from Triesch – now in the Czech Republic and called Třešť – to Graz. Then she married a retired general, thirty years her senior, so her son could go to an even better school: the elite Theresianum in Vienna. He studied in the city too, being awarded his PhD at the age of twenty-three. At twenty-four he married his first wife, and at twenty-five he produced his first major work, *The Nature and Essence of Economic Theory*. The title is a reflection of Schumpeter's remarkable confidence, at a time when many older professors only wrote analyses that were nothing more than descriptions of certain economic sectors during certain periods. Schumpeter on the other hand – like Thünen – aims for abstraction, which allows mathematical methods to be applied and general theorems to be formulated; he considers the natural sciences to be a discipline closely related to economics, rather than sociology or psychology.

He got his first chair at twenty-seven in Czernowitz, now Chernivtsi in Ukraine, where he did in fact have a duel with the librarian – but not over a woman. Schumpeter had been so vehement in his demand for students to have better access to the books that his adversary challenged him to a duel. Schumpeter was the better of two inexperienced swordsmen and wounded his opponent on the shoulder, which allowed the man's second to abort the fight.

In 1911 Schumpeter became professor in Graz and finished the work that would make him famous: *The Theory of Economic*

Development. The wavelike ups and downs of the economic cycle are more complicated than a water wave. What happens to the glassy surface of the water in an aquarium if we drop a stone in or tip the aquarium? Amongst physicists dealing with fluid dynamics this question does not trigger a heated controversy. They can calculate what occurs because the water molecules don't pursue any interests of their own.

By contrast, arguments over models of the economic cycle are unlikely to end because they have to deal with the fact that 'molecules', i.e. consumers and businesses, think about what is best for themselves and what the future might hold. Is further investment worthwhile? Should I buy a car or save the money? Economic models differ in their assumptions of how such decisions are taken. They also differ in their opinions as to which stone triggers the wave in the first place. For Schumpeter it is innovation – a new project, a new manufacturing process, new sales channels, some entrepreneur seizing an opportunity and obtaining large profits, followed by imitators who earn even more, as do the workforce (who become in short supply in some careers and sectors) and suppliers. At some point, however, the innovation no longer provides any particular advantages. Those who still expect some will be disappointed, credit will need to be repaid and the downturn begins, although the trajectory doesn't lead back to the starting position, which is another difference between the business cycle and water waves.

Schumpeter's theory didn't become widely accepted (his

550-page book is hardly ever read these days), with one exception. He devotes fifty pages to a realistic depiction of the entrepreneur. (Prior to this, economic theory gave little consideration to the entrepreneur, who was simply the person who owned the means of production and who reaped the profits.) But what does 'realistic' mean in this context? In truth it is a magic mirror, in which every reader sees their own image of the entrepreneur and entrepreneurship.

Anyone who regards entrepreneurs as the true bearers of progress, those who aren't specifically inventors but who convert inventions into improvements for society, or at least for consumers, can feel validated by Schumpeter. Without entrepreneurs, he writes, inventions are as 'meaningless as the canals on Mars'.

Those who see entrepreneurs as destroyers, ruthless agents of change, usurpers who ruin what is familiar for their own success, will also feel validated. When Schumpeter describes entrepreneurs as 'real blokes', we can interpret this either as ridicule or as a paean to macho men – cleverly, Schumpeter lets the reader make up their own mind.

We also find the irrational entrepreneur who acts completely uneconomically, because what else can be acquired that would justify the expenditure of more time and energy? It's hard to explain without a 'thirst for action', the pleasure of power and creation.

Schumpeter's own thirst for action was not quenched by his early academic success. The next ten years sound like the muddled scribblings of a writer on drugs – too many bizarre things happen.

In 1916 in Graz, Schumpeter – the man who boasted of his amorous escapades and made notes about women in his diaries as if he were on the jury of an endless top model competition – supported the right of women to finally study law.

Schumpeter, who opposed the war, sent memoranda to influential noblemen advocating that Austria-Hungary should make a separate peace with the Allies. The peace that eventually resulted was economically difficult for the new Republic of Austria, which had inherited too many officials and too many debts from the unwieldy old Monarchy. Schumpeter became its first finance minister in 1919.

In this office he was disadvantaged by his much-vaunted ability for not only taking on board other people's viewpoints, but occasionally even championing them himself. The socialists, for example, seriously believed that Schumpeter supported their ideas on the nationalisation of certain industries, but he didn't. He didn't make any friends among the conservatives either. Schumpeter called for a one-off capital levy to settle the country's debts. He conspired with Anna Sacher (the owner of Hotel Sacher in Vienna) and Max von Neumann (the banker and father of John von Neumann) to provide support for the Hungarian opposition, who ultimately brought down the communist government there. And he was the only member of the Austrian government to reject outright an Anschluss with Germany.

Very soon, therefore, he found himself almost without friends politically. He got on the nerves of Viennese society with his ostentatiously luxurious lifestyle and unconventional love affairs (his longest relationship was with a prostitute, who styled herself 'Nelly Schumpeter'). After only seven months he had to give up his position as finance minister.

But there was a silver lining: Schumpeter obtained a bank licence, making him an attractive partner for an associate who was rich but without a licence. In 1921 he became president of the private Biedermann Bank. This venture only lasted for a few years. Schumpeter was not a born private banker; he bought and sold ineptly, trusted the wrong people, and was forced to resign even before the bank became insolvent in 1924. Compensation to the tune of his annual salary was not enough to settle his personal debts, and before long the small fortune he'd acquired in 1907 and 1908 for successfully managing the assets of an Egyptian princess had dried up. Here ends the novel.

Schumpeter returned to research and, by means of publications and lectures, gradually made a dent in his mountain of debt, which was several times what most professors earned in a year. Then he found the love of his life. Annie was a young office worker, daughter of his mother's caretaker, which disappointed Frau Schumpeter as she'd hoped for someone more befitting her son's social status. In 1925 Schumpeter accepted a chair at the University of Bonn and married Annie, which almost saw him prosecuted for bigamy as he hadn't yet divorced his first wife (in practice, the marriage hadn't existed for more than ten years).

In 1926 he was dealt two cruel blows by fate. His beloved mother, to whom he owed so much, died of an aneurysm, and his wife Annie died in childbirth (the baby itself only lived for a few hours). For the rest of his life Schumpeter would address a sort of prayer to the two dead women, whom he called the 'rabbits'. Here, for example, is an extract from his diary:

Harvard, Mon 23rd – Sun 29th Oct 33

... I take my leave of this week and month, which has flown past so quicky and not been unhappy, with humble grati-tude to the rabbits who have helped me so much more than I deserve.

Yes, Harvard. The university recruited him in 1932, which meant his emigration wasn't a case of political expulsion and flight. He fared better than most exiles, as he had no diffi-culty with the language, writing English and giving lectures effortlessly. His first wife had been British and he'd already undertaken research trips to London, Cambridge, Oxford, New York, and Harvard.

But Schumpeter wasn't happy. Increasingly he buried himself in his academic work, so it was no surprise when he married a fellow economist he met in Harvard. Nonetheless, he still turned to the 'rabbits'; in 1942, even though he'd now been married to Elizabeth for five years, he noted:

Over the past year, there is no doubt that I have descended towards old age, and even more directly towards death. My heart, my brain, my limbs, everything is disappearing ... I do not know if there is much I can do to stop this, nor if I even wish to. The only prayer I offer up to the rabbits and to God is that it should end gently, not in horrible operations, paralysis and lingering illness. O, grant me this mercy!

Although he was also depressed by the war, Schumpeter continued to be productive and successful. His greatest accomplishment was a peripheral piece of work he didn't consider to be important, written originally in English and which has since been translated into at least fifteen languages: *Capitalism, Socialism and Democracy*. Schumpeter described it as a 'book of essays', and in truth the five parts of the book don't hang that closely together; each can happily be read on its own. The first section remains one of the most readable introductions to Marxist economics. He wins over non-Marxist readers to Marx in three ways. First, he assures them that 'between the true meaning of Marx's message and bolshevist practice and ideology [there is] at least as great a gulf as there was between the religion of humble Galileans and the practice and ideology of the princes of the church or the warlords of the Middle Ages'. Second, he translates Marxist terminology into more familiar language, which greatly facilitates the reading for those who don't have *Das Kapital* on their bedside table. And third, he praises Marx for his analysis of the huge progress that capitalist entrepreneurs have made. He quotes approvingly from Marx and Engels's writings on the bourgeoisie in *The Communist Manifesto*: '[It] has been the first to show what man's activity can bring about. It has accomplished wonders far surpassing Egyptian pyramids, Roman aqueducts and Gothic cathedrals.' They go on: 'The bourgeoisie, during its rule of scarce 100 years, has created more massive and more colossal productive forces than have all preceding generations together.'

Although Schumpeter clearly admires Marx as an analyst, he disagrees with him on a few fundamental points. He criticises Marx's crisis theory and theory of collapse, which states that more and more workers will be replaced by machines, and that an increasing number of small businesses won't be able to keep up with this process. Schumpeter laments Marx's lack of imagination, which fails to see that new entrepreneurs with new products and new technological processes will be able take the place of the old ones; capitalism is not about the big eating up the small, but the new replacing the old. Even if you know nothing about Schumpeter, you'll have heard the name he gave this phenomenon in his book: 'creative destruction'.

All the same, Schumpeter doesn't believe we can take capitalism's survival for granted. In the second part he sketches his own theories about the possible end of capitalism. Businesses are not killed off by dwindling profits, but instead they adapt. In the past there were a lot of small and medium businesses in which the entrepreneur was both owner and manager. With his charismatic influence on the foremen, he served as a walking argument for private ownership. The perception of businesses and entrepreneurs changes, however, when they are replaced by firms run by employed managers rather than the proprietors. Schumpeter admits that these businesses also have a huge capacity for innovation, but he says, 'Even if the giant concerns were all managed so perfectly as to call forth applause from the angels in heaven' the political consequences of this development would still be inevitable: nobody outside the huge firms would be prepared to speak up for capitalism. Just as the power of kings and popes was unable to maintain the old order, private ownership and the 'whole scheme of bourgeois values' cannot be preserved. Schumpeter leaves open the question as to whether socialism will creep out of gradual bureaucratisation or from 'the most picturesque revolution', or maybe not at all, for he operates scientifically, and describes a tendency, not a prophecy. At all events Schumpeter had good reason to question in the next section of his book whether socialism can work.

During his tenure as finance minister, the Viennese *Arbeiter-Zeitung* was 'astonished' at how 'Schumpeter was always able to tailor his speeches to the audience: before the workers' council he almost spoke like a social democrat and at the farmer's conference he sounded just like an agriculturalist'. As far as the social-democratic newspaper was concerned this indicated a lack of principles, a view shared by Karl Kraus, who described him as a 'visiting professor of his convictions'. But it's also possible to see a talent in this adaptability. In this respect Schumpeter's answer to the question 'Can socialism work?', which he gives in *Capitalism, Socialism and Democracy*, is the most glittering proof of his talent. He doesn't need different speeches to convince one camp followed by the other. On the contrary, he can appear as a socialist to the socialists and a conservative to the conservatives in the same text.

Schumpeter achieves this with the use of irony. The use of irony in scholarship goes back at least as far as Socrates, but it is rare. Those who are being ironic don't mean what they write. Most academics, by contrast, want to write exactly what they mean. This is a hard enough task in itself, and they believe that ironic élan is too costly if it leaves the text open to misunderstanding.

With Socrates the matter is fairly clear. When in the Theaetetus dialogue he says: 'it is not a bad description of knowledge that you have given, but one which Protagoras also used to give ... It is likely that a wise man is not talking nonsense', he doesn't really mean it – for since when did Socrates believe the authorship of an argument guarantees its validity? But what should the reader, who isn't prepared for something like this, think when Schumpeter agrees with the economist Enrico Barone, claiming that Barone has solved all the key problems of socialism: the production plants would belong to a central authority, which merely has to set the internal prices for raw materials and everything else the factories need to ensure the 'markets are cleared', meaning that neither too much nor too little is produced. Theoretically this isn't a problem. In practice it's certainly a challenge for the bureaucracy, but there are advantages too, he says, such as the end of uncertainty over what the competition will do. Savings can also be made on the costs of the lawyers who the entrepreneurs would have previously hired to fight against the state and its organs, and these lawyers are given something productive to do instead.

For readers who knew nothing about Schumpeter save for this book, the above may not have appeared particularly ironic. But he makes himself clearer later on: if income disappears as an incentive for performance, perhaps it can be replaced by a penny stamp that the successful individual sticks on their trousers. If the stamp creates sufficient prestige, it will have fulfilled its purpose. And even if less is produced under socialism – which does not have to be the case – this doesn't mean that fewer needs are satisfied, for staunch socialists prefer the taste of socialist bread, and they would still do so 'even if they found mice in it'. And workers wouldn't go on strike anymore, at least not without feeling bad about their antisocial assault on society's prosperity.

In short, socialism won't work, but could come about nonetheless. Maybe not until capitalism is ripe for it, and when the large concerns, which are bureaucratic anyway, become socialist enterprises through a simple change in constitution. But maybe socialism will emerge when it's in a state of 'unpreparedness' or when 'things and souls' are still immature, in which case a revolution will be needed. Another reason for Schumpeter to be depressed and feel that he no longer belonged in this world. In December 1948, after a successful speech he gave as president of the American Economic Association, he noted in his diary:

> Thanks, rabbits, for your support and for one of the richest gifts. Everyone got to their feet for my president's speech … Thank you, rabbits. O give me strength. O God and rabbits. And allow me slowly to get used to the idea of a death by choice. Should I say, help me to a death by choice? O God and rabbits, thanks. Bless 1949 if that is your wish. I cannot wait much more than another year.

This was an accurate prediction. But Schumpeter wasn't anxious; in his diaries, at any rate, he had time and again begged the rabbits:

> Help me gently into my grave.

This they did on 8 January 1950. They didn't show much imagination as far as cause of death was concerned. Just like his mother, Schumpeter died of an aneurysm.

9

Von Neumann and the Price of Nuclear Deterrence

JOHN VON NEUMANN
1903–1957

It is an indubitable fact that John von Neumann died; his last days are well documented. A lieutenant colonel kept vigil in his death chamber, lest he reveal any state secrets in his delirium. But did an economist die with John von Neumann? He certainly made an important contribution to economics, if only incidentally, but it would have been sufficient to win him a Nobel Prize in Economics had he been old enough. Nor did any one discipline have an exclusive claim on him: not physics, not computer science – not even mathematics.

John von Neumann was born in Budapest in 1903. When he was still small and called János, he believed that everyone else was hardwired like him. When his mother once broke off from her needlework and stared thoughtfully into space, he asked, 'What are you calculating?' He wasn't just a maths genius – he also had a phenomenal memory. It is a known fact that he could recite the opening pages of Dickens's novel *A Tale of Two*

Cities by heart. At twenty-three he already had three academic degrees: in chemistry from the University of Budapest, where he only turned up to take the exams; in chemical engineering from Zurich; and a PhD in mathematics from Budapest again.

His first mathematical publications soon followed, even the titles of which are unintelligible to the layperson, such as *On Prüfer's Theory of Ideal Numbers* and *General Eigenvalue Theory of Hermitian Functional Operators*. In 1928, however, he wrote a paper in German entitled *On the Theory of Games of Strategy*, in which he solved a problem that had stumped two major thinkers of the time.

The first was Emanuel Lasker, a doctor in mathematics and World Chess Champion from 1894 to 1921. At the end of the 1920s he was earning his money giving bridge lessons. In his book *Encyclopedia of Games, Volume One: Card Strategy* he sought to find an optimal strategy for poker. He believed he'd come to grips at least with the much-simplified two-person poker game he called 'pokerette'. Assuming there are only thirteen different cards, the rules of this poker are as follows: the two players get a card with a number between 1 and 13. Each must then decide whether they're going to bet they have a higher number than the other player. Lasker works out very long-windedly that the first player should bet if they have a 9 or higher, and pass if their card has a lower face value. But what about bluffing – betting on a low card in the hope the other person will fold? For Lasker this is an irrational move that can't pay off when the game is played sensibly.

Here Lasker was wrong. Occasionally it's necessary to bluff, for otherwise your opponent will of course know the minimum value of your card when they bet. John von Neumann was able to show that it's important and right to make yourself unpredictable by bluffing from time to time.

Meanwhile, the young economist Oskar Morgenstern was racking his brains over a problem of economic prognosis – one that is fortunately alien to the natural sciences. A solar eclipse occurs whether we predict it or not. An economic forecast, on the other hand, has an impact on the economy itself. If a 5 per cent increase in investment is predicted, this forecast can boost the increase to 10 per cent. What to do? Should the effect of the prognosis be accounted for in the prognosis itself? Doesn't this in turn have an effect that ought to be predicted?

In one of Conan Doyle's Sherlock Holmes stories Morgenstern finds an analogy that, in his view, demonstrates the problem is unsolvable:

Sherlock Holmes is fleeing from his arch-rival Professor Moriarty, who as well as being evil and dangerous is also so intelligent as to be a match for the master detective. Holmes is sitting on a train to Dover, having planned to take the ferry from there to France. He realises, however, that Moriarty must have seen him at the station. With an express train Moriarty could be in Dover before Holmes; this would spell the end of the detective, as his adversary would be waiting for him at his destination. But because Holmes can predict that Moriarty will be travelling to Dover, he could get out at Canterbury, the only stop en route. Moriarty in turn might anticipate this and go to Canterbury himself, rather than Dover. In which case, Moriarty... and so on. Whether or not Holmes thinks that getting out at Canterbury or Dover is the more intelligent choice, his equally intelligent opponent will be lying in wait for him. The search for a better strategy appears pointless.

Ten years later, however, Oskar Morgenstern discovered that John von Neumann had in his paper described a method that could offer a solution to this problem. The two academics had ended up as émigrés in Princeton, giving Morgenstern the opportunity to persuade Neumann that they should work on a book together. *Theory of Games and Economic Behavior* appeared in 1944, revolutionising at a stroke the analysis of cooperation and conflict; ever since, game theory has been indispensable to economic research. It's needed to answer questions such as: can small groups of businesses keep the price artificially high in their sector? Or do they need to trick each other by cutting prices? Should a firm manufacture a component itself, or can it rely on buying a good-quality version from other companies?

Neumann and Morgenstern didn't address these questions themselves; instead they developed the tools with which to do so in the first place. They did, however, solve Holmes's problem, quite incidentally. Just as when playing poker you shouldn't *always* bluff, or refrain from doing so altogether, Holmes ought to set a certain probability for getting out at Canterbury. He could, for example, use dice to determine what he does. Then it doesn't matter how smart Moriarty is – he won't be able to predict how the dice falls and he'll only catch his enemy if he's lucky.

It was typical of John von Neumann to be interested in mathematical problems that arose (or might arise) in real life. He liked listening to the radio as he worked, loved parties, and often invited people over. He was a friendly, attentive host, even though he would occasionally leave his guests on their own for an hour or two while he went back to his desk. He enjoyed driving, despite having a reputation for being a terrible driver, or at least a reckless one. Around one car per year fell victim to his escapades behind the wheel, and a street corner in Princeton, the scene of many of these misadventures, was known by insiders as 'Von Neumann Corner'.

For most economists von Neumann is the man who made a decisive impact on modern economics with his game theory (Oskar Morgenstern is generally credited with having encouraged von Neumann to come up with this). Far less well known is his mathematical model of a growing economy, which since its publication in 1937 has been admired by the few experts who understand it, but otherwise has had little influence. In any case, with this theoretical work von Neumann had no intention of helping or influencing practical policy.

Military historians know quite a different John von Neumann, one who researched detonation waves and assisted the Ballistic Research Laboratory. Most notably, however, while still working on his game theory book, he acted as a mathematical adviser to the Manhattan Project, which developed the atomic bomb. With nuclear weapons there's very little you can test in the laboratory, so the US benefited greatly from the fact that von Neumann was able to perform a wealth of calculations. He was also a member of the nine-man targeting committee that chose Hiroshima and Nagasaki for the first two atomic bombs. It's impossible to put a precise figure on the number of deaths (later estimated at 200,000); as a result, Japan was forced to surrender.

The development of the atomic bomb was not a controversial issue amongst American scientists, as the fear that Hitler might get hold of this weapon first was too great.

And this fear didn't end with the Second World War. In 1949 the Soviet Union carried out the first nuclear test. In the US, some scientists were by now calling for disarmament and a control on nuclear weapons. They were opposed by the hardliners, of whom von Neumann was one – even during the war he'd regarded the Soviet Union as an enemy rather than an ally. Von Neumann was the son of a wealthy banker – in 1919 the family had been forced to leave Budapest for a few months, fleeing from the Hungarian Soviet government. This government, and the family's exile at their holiday home on the Adriatic, lasted only a few months, but it was a defining experience for the fifteen-year-old János. Even at the age of fifty he would say, 'I think you will find, generally speaking, among Hungarians an emotional fear and dislike of Russia.'

If it had been up to von Neumann, the US would have

launched a pre-emptive nuclear strike on the Soviet Union to avoid being attacked themselves. Although this idea never made headway, von Neumann remained a respected adviser on armaments policy and nuclear research. He was involved in the development of the hydrogen bomb, which could unleash 1,000 times the destructive energy of the atomic bomb.

Von Neumann loved his work for the military, which was not merely down to a patriotic bond with his new homeland, but also his sometimes childish, almost schoolboyish nature. He would uninhibitedly try to look up the skirts of the secretaries who worked at the atomic research centre in Los Alamos. He was as excited by technological toys as he was by uniforms, or the army helicopter that occasionally picked him up from the institute. How could this man possibly turn down the offer to observe a nuclear weapons test on Bikini Atoll in 1946?

We'll never know if von Neumann would have lived longer had he not been subjected to the heightened radiation. We do know, however, that he was precisely aware of the radiation risk from nuclear technology and thought it was acceptable, especially in the context of the 30,000–40,000 fatal motor accidents per year, which was the price the US paid for the convenience of car travel. During another test on Bikini Atoll in 1954, a miscalculation meant that the explosive power released by the hydrogen bomb was two-and-a-half times greater than anticipated; at the same time, the wind changed direction. A Japanese fisherman on the cutter 'Lucky Dragon' got caught in the blast and died as a result, and 200 people were exposed to radiation. Von Neumann pointed out, however, that although around 1,000 people had died in a Japanese ferry disaster that same year, including twenty Americans, it was the radioactive fallout that received worldwide attention. The loss of international popularity was a price that the US should pay, in his view.

In 1955 he learned he had bone cancer. It's hard to say what was worse for John von Neumann – the pain or the feeling that his intellectual powers were waning once the cancer started attacking his brain (although while in hospital with his brother, he was still able to recite passages from *Faust* unforgotten from his German lessons at school). Nothing could mitigate the dread of his impending death – not the Medal of Freedom he was given in his wheelchair by President Eisenhower, nor his view that God probably existed because that made many things much easier to explain. Nor did it help when, on his deathbed, he converted to Catholicism and requested to talk to a priest who was a match for him intellectually. He died on 8 February 1957 at the age of fifty-three.

10

Schmölders' Dream of America

GÜNTER SCHMÖLDERS
1903–1991

What happens at the end of the twentieth century when a professor dies after many years in retirement? Roughly this: for a certain period of mourning his study at home remains as it was. But then, after a few months or years, his widow begins to feel the weight of all that paper. Books, loose academic periodicals, bound periodicals, typewritten dissertations, files with minutes of meetings. What to do with them? She decides altruistically to bequeath the papers to the university. In the deceased's address book she finds the number of Dr W., the head of the university archive. Dr W. doesn't answer, but instead she gets through to someone who had no idea his telephone number was linked to an archive. He doesn't even think such an archive exists. He offers to do a quick search for 'archive' on the university's website. When it brings up no results he gives the astonished widow the telephone number of the dean of the faculty; maybe she'll be happy to look after the papers.

The widow wonders whether in her long life she's ever heard of a female dean before, and eventually makes the call. It turns out the dean has never heard of the dead man. His widow nonetheless explains what she's proposing to offer. The dean then explains why the faculty isn't interested: there isn't the space and, in any case, the offprints her husband collected are no longer needed because all these papers are now available to download as pdfs. The Samuelson, for example, might be a standard work, but there are plenty of copies of it in the library, and in more modern editions. Times have changed. On the dean's recommendation, the widow contacts an antiquarian bookseller who comes to the house and offers a three-figure sum for a four-figure number of books, but on the condition he doesn't have to take the rest of the papers. The strongest of the five grandchildren takes these to the recycling centre.

This sort of thing has happened hundreds of times. A researcher's papers aren't interesting unless the researcher is really important. If they are, they get a choice as to where these papers end up. Günter Schmölders had the choice; he didn't leave it up to his descendants. In his lifetime his papers amounted to 176 boxes of manuscripts the size of wine crates. Schmölders was extremely industrious, producing around fifty books (for which he carefully assembled all the reviews) and more than 400 articles. Six years before his death he had them sent to America, to the Hoover Institution at Stanford University. This was a strange choice, as most Americans couldn't make use of the bequest. Only one short book and sixteen of the articles had been written by Schmölders in English, most of the latter only being a few sides long. This was a huge obstacle, which nobody helped him to surmount: 'My books have been translated into Turkish, Japanese, Korean, Italian, French, and countless other languages, but never into English,' he complained.

Nowadays economic research is conducted exclusively in English, but in Schmölders' time things were different. When in 1928 the *Jahrbücher für Nationalökonomie und Statistik (Journal of Economics and Statistics)*, already back then a venerable publication, published his essay 'Criminality and Economic Conditions', not only was each of the six papers in German, but not a single one referenced an English-language source. Schmölders would have found it hard to do so, as in 1928 he could barely speak a word of English. He didn't begin teaching himself until August of that year with the help of his *Langenscheidt* dictionary, making good use of the eleven days the steamer took to get to New York from Germany.

He had a decent foundation for picking up the new language, having learned Latin, Greek, French, and Norwegian in his youth, and he may also have inherited some of his grandfather's talent (an orientalist with a knowledge of twenty-two languages, this man needed three replacements at the University of Breslau when he died in 1880). But eleven days is a pitifully short time, and Schmölders found the pronunciation impossible to master – hardly surprising for a language where 'wine' doesn't rhyme with 'magazine' and 'beer' rhymes with 'hear' but not 'bear'.

Schmölders did not cross the Atlantic to discuss his research with American academics. Two years earlier he'd been awarded his doctorate on alcohol prohibition in Sweden, and now he was going to embark on a major study of the causes and economic effects of prohibition in the US.

He was lucky. At the time of his research trip, the problems associated with the alcohol ban were already evident. The available statistics were not ideal: some cities classified as drunk those people who couldn't say 'Wesleyan Methodist' properly, while elsewhere more classic indicators had been used, such as unsteady walking and boozy breath. Nonetheless, Schmölders used what was at his disposal, and in the end he was able to come up with a pretty clear picture. When prohibition came into force in 1920 it appeared to have a positive impact: less alcohol was indeed consumed, there were fewer arrests for drunkenness, and a lower mortality rate connected to alcoholism. But then came illegal production, speakeasies, and smuggling. The side effects of alcoholism almost returned to previous levels. In addition to this, Schmölders observed some ugly side effects common to every black economy. Inferior substitutes had started to appear, in this case chiefly methanol, which killed or blinded many poor souls. The incentives to bribe and be bribed were huge: every honest official working for the prohibition authority in Philadelphia, Schmölders calculated, cost the moonshiners $10 million per year, but only earned $2,000 themselves. Of course, the judiciary didn't intervene to protect the black marketeers, so agreements and power struggles were carried out with force. Schmölders witnessed this close up when an explosion woke him from his sleep. A bomb planted by rivals had destroyed the speakeasy right beside his hotel.

There are many reasons why prohibition lasted so long – until 1933 – despite these downsides, and why the ban came about in the first place. Schmölders was particularly caustic while tracing the role of Protestantism: 'puritanical in its reasoning and morality, fanatical and intolerant to the point of absurdity in its battle against religious indifference and alien, modern ideas.' The personal decision of whether to drink alcohol had become quasi-religious: anyone who had taken a 'vow of abstinence' was a 'convert'.

In addition, the brewing industry recruited among Germans, or those with German heritage, whose lobby suffered accordingly during the First World War. Moreover, politicians who personally had no inclination towards abstinence often supported prohibition nonetheless, either because they thought alcohol-related problems afflicted workers and black people, or for tactical electoral reasons. These, at any rate, were the premises Schmölders worked with to understand the policy. In the second half of the twentieth century this method, known as the 'economic theory of policy' or Public Choice, became an important branch of economic research. Not for the last time would Schmölders be ahead of his time.

What he published during the National Socialist era,

however, comes across as strikingly uninspired. The texts he wrote by himself are at least free from Nazi jargon, but this is not always the case for papers he co-authored (with his colleague, Alfons Schmitt, he complained shortly before the war of the 'political agitation' by 'so-called' democracies such as the US against the sale of German goods, but suggests that after the 'creation of the Greater German Reich and the collapse of the Czecho-Slovak buffer state', export policy could at least become established in south-eastern Europe, 'in many respects the natural area of influence and hinterland of the Greater German economy').

By joining the Nazi Party, Schmölders avoided disruptions to his career. His first professorship in Breslau in 1934 was followed by a chair in Cologne. Soon afterwards, however, he became a member of the Kreisau Circle led by Helmuth James von Moltke and Peter Graf Yorck von Wartenburg, a resistance group who, in their meetings, discussed how they might reorganise the social order after the toppling of the National Socialist regime. Schmölders acted as an economic adviser and was earmarked for future office in the finance ministry. His military service saved him from the fate of arrest and execution which ultimately befell some members of the group.

After the war there were a few German economists whose work gained an international reputation. These were almost exclusively amongst the 200-or-so economists who went into exile after 1933, most to the USA. Very few returned to Germany. So where was inspiration to come from? It's no wonder German universities in the 1950s produced little economic research of note. There were exceptions, of course – individual plants on dry, sandy soils. Heinz Sauermann, for example, who was one of the first to observe and analyse how people behaved in systematic economic experiments. Another exception was Günter Schmölders.

To understand his importance it is essential to know that although economists of the time looked at consumers and other actors in the economy, they dealt with model reconstructions rather than real scenarios. Researchers assumed that firms and consumers (later politicians and bureaucrats too) always tried to pursue their goals in optimal fashion, and they contemplated how they themselves would do this instead of consumers and managers. The British economist Ely Devons explained it like this: 'Suppose an economist wanted to study the horse. What would he do? He would go to his study and ask himself, what would I do if I were a horse?'

Schmölders, by contrast, asked how people actually came to their economic decisions. To do this he had them surveyed on the subjects of saving, getting into debt, the tax burden (on this point perception rarely corresponded with reality), and tax compliance. He pulled off a particular coup in 1958, when he was able to question all twenty-seven members of the finance committee as well as a representative cross-section of German parliamentarians, which came to ninety-two politicians overall.

Many of his questions, unfortunately, are fairly specific to the time. From 1953 to 1957, most notably in 1956, the state achieved budget surpluses. A hotly debated issue was what to do with these surpluses. Disburse them? The additional demand could lead to inflation. Leave them permanently with the central bank, i.e. take them out of the finance minister's hands forever? Many members of parliament couldn't get their heads round the idea that 'destroying money' doesn't necessarily make an economy poorer. In fact what happened is this: the surpluses were set aside temporarily, but spent later. This turned out to be the model for counter-cyclical economic policy whereby the state steps in as consumer when the economy is sluggish, and holds back during an economic boom with high tax receipts. Schmölders, however, thought it was a lucky coincidence that this policy worked so well in the late 1950s. Most members of parliament hadn't understood the economics behind it. Those who weren't economic experts came to their conclusions not through analysis but slogans: 'Money has to work', 'Money sensualises', 'Healthy breathing space', or 'The money must stay in the economy' – Schmölders called this 'stamped passes for ... standardised thoughts and feelings'. He didn't, however, criticise the politicians, arguing that modern life in general called for conceptual abbreviations by means of 'pre-determined formulae'. Forty years later such abbreviations, known as 'heuristics', became a popular subject of research within psychological economics.

Economically Schmölders may have been a revolutionary, or at least a pioneer, but politically he was a conservative. A friendly remark that Konrad Adenauer once made to him at a state reception – 'Did you make it OK?' – Schmölders later used as the title of his autobiography. The book is a rather dry reflection upon his academic career, although his account of his research trip to the US is one of the livelier sections and worth reading. His experiences of prohibition are portrayed as amongst the most formative of his life; he saw it as a key example of how state intervention can have a different outcome from what was intended.

Schmölders died in 1991 at the age of eighty-eight, and like many people who reach such a ripe old age, he saw things change. The *Journal of Economics and Statistics* now has an English title, all the articles are in English, and practically all the literature referred to is in English as well. Just as in 1928 a German professor could get by with German alone, nowadays English alone suffices. Many younger, German-speaking economists haven't published a single line of research in German.

At the most important annual meeting of German economists a prize named after Schmölders is awarded every year. In America, by contrast, he remains unknown. There seems to be no rational explanation as to why he should have sent his papers to America, but the decision was typical of the man, who paved the way for psychology to enter into economic research. But what he never achieved – success in America – is something his papers haven't been blessed with either. Only once every decade does someone in the Hoover Institution request to look in one of his 176 boxes.

11

Vickrey's Very Brief Delight at the Nobel Prize

WILLIAM VICKREY
1914–1996

One fine day in the mid-1960s William Vickrey stuck a transmitter under the bonnet of his car. In his house he attached a matching receiver to a primitive computer, which recorded when the car left the driveway or returned, and occasionally he printed out the data. This wasn't just a gimmick. Vickrey wanted to demonstrate how car drivers can be charged for road use without making them stop at tolls. Vickrey couldn't bear tolls. Although they have a positive aim – reducing the number of cars on the roads and thus preventing traffic jams – they achieve the opposite: tailbacks at barriers.

But what did Vickrey have against traffic jams? He was a neo-classical economist who assumed that people acted rationally and pursued their objectives as best they could. Anyone who drives in New York at eight in the morning knows that they're going to make slow progress. If they drive nonetheless, they implicitly accept the price in the form of the time it will cost them. They believe therefore that the journey is worthwhile. Where's the problem? Don't neo-classicists believe that the decisions made by each individual car driver will magically lead to the optimum outcome? No, most of them don't believe this, even though it's always said they do. The problem is that a car driver at rush hour doesn't bear all the costs they incur; they also burden those people behind them with additional waiting time. If everyone pursues the optimal solution for themselves, the result is not the best outcome for society – far from it. So what should be done?

Vickrey was an advocate of 'peak load prices', prices that are higher when more people want to use the road. This ensures that the roads are no longer congested because some car owners adjust their leaving times accordingly. For anyone who doesn't absolutely have to drive at eight in the morning, it's worth waiting until ten or eleven o'clock, or even not using the car at all. Vickrey himself demonstrated that this worked: irritated by jams he would usually take the train most of the way to the university, and then roller-skate from the station at 116th Street to the campus.

He's not only remembered by his colleagues as a roller-skater. Every faculty has a professor who nods off during lectures, or appears to nod off, but who afterwards asks the most pertinent questions. At Columbia University this professor was William Vickrey. His capacity to switch off like this won him a 'Rip van Winkle Award', named after the protagonist of Washington Irving's short story, who falls into a magical twenty-year sleep as a citizen of the English colony of New York, and wakes up in the US. Vickrey, however, was without a doubt ahead of his time; many of his ideas weren't understood and acknowledged until decades later.

He was eighty-two when, on 8 October 1996, he found out that together with James Mirrlees he'd won the Nobel Prize in Economics, for 'their fundamental contributions to the economic theory of incentives under asymmetric information'. When a friend rang to congratulate him, he admitted he wasn't sure which of his works this related to, and seemed more interested in what his friend was working on at that moment, and how his family were faring. What's certain, however, is that Vickrey was awarded the prize for his older mathematical research.

An example of an economic problem that can't be solved without maths is a sealed-bid auction. Imagine that a painting you like is being auctioned in this way. You write your bid on a piece of paper and pass it to the auctioneer. The other bidders do the same. When the auctioneer has gathered all the bids, the person who has offered the most gets the picture. The price is what they wrote on the piece of paper.

Let's say your 'pain threshold' is €1,000. By 'pain threshold' we mean that if the painting were on sale in a shop for €1,000 you would buy it, but not at €1,001. (Economists have no problem in calling this pain threshold a 'valuation'.)

But you're not in a shop: you're wondering how much to bid in this auction. €1,000? If so, will you really be happy if you win the auction? That price is your pain threshold. Less, then. €900? €800? The less you offer, the greater your delight if you win, but the lower the probability *that* you will win. You don't know what the others are going to bid; at best you might have an inkling of the probability of different bids. For Vickrey such hunches are sufficient to calculate the optimal offer for each bidder and what sum the auctioneer can hope to earn. He also showed that different auction rules are neither better nor worse for the auctioneer.

Here is an example of different rules. Once again, each person writes down their bid, and once again the auctioneer picks out the highest offer, but the winner doesn't pay the sum they wrote on their piece of paper. The price is only as high as the *second-highest* bid. Nowadays these auctions are known as 'Vickrey auctions', even though they existed before Vickrey analysed them.

You might think that in a Vickrey auction, the auctioneer is losing out. On the contrary, under this new rule all bids come out higher. Consider again the painting that's worth €1,000, as far as you're concerned. Is it now sensible to bid €900? No, it is not. Let's assume €900 is enough to win the auction because the second-highest bid is only €800. How much will you pay? In a Vickrey auction, €800 – the same you would have paid if you'd bid €1,000. If, however, someone bids €950 and you bid only €900, you'll be annoyed. The painting is now someone else's. If you'd offered €1,000 you would have got it for €950, still comfortably beneath your pain threshold.

This is the funny thing about Vickrey auctions. Everyone bids exactly what they think the item being auctioned is worth. For the bid only influences whether you win the item, not how much you pay for it. (If you offer more than €1,000, however, it can backfire because the second-highest bid could be over €1,000 too, in which case you've done a bad deal.)

It's clear, therefore, that the *bids* at a Vickrey auction end up higher than if every winner were to pay what they bid. This idea alone, however, wasn't what earned him the Nobel Prize; Vickrey's stellar achievement was calculating that the *prices* for items under the two different rules will be, on average, exactly the same. This is also true, incidentally, for an 'English auction', which works in the way most people imagine an auction to be. It begins with a low sum and those interested in the item keep bidding over each other until there's only one left – going once, going twice, going three times, bang! The auctioneer can also begin at a very high price and lower the figure incrementally until someone shouts 'stop' and buys at the last-mentioned price. Because fish and tulip bulbs have been auctioned this way in the Netherlands for ages, it's known as a 'Dutch auction'.

Anyone after a few thrills can now buy all manner of things on the internet through Dutch auctions. And where will you find a Vickrey auction? If you make a bid on eBay you usually enter the highest sum you're willing to pay at that moment. If you win the auction, it will be because by using eBay's automatic bidding system you've outbid all the others, often only by a small sum – the minimum increase necessary. What price do you pay? Just a few cents more than the second highest bid. You've won a Vickrey auction.

While Vickrey claimed that the financial aspect of the Nobel Prize meant little to him, he welcomed the opportunity to give a speech about what he was currently working on, which was no longer mathematical models of individual actors in specific markets. At the end of his career he was interested in macro-economic problems, especially unemployment, and he had returned to his old favourite topic of taxation – although 'favourite topic of taxation' possibly gives a false impression. While a couple of corporate types were waffling on about income tax at some conference, Vickrey sat there doing a crossword puzzle. When the time came for questions Vickrey asked, 'Don't you think you're just rearranging deck chairs on the Titanic?'

By contrast, Vickrey was after a comprehensive reform of the tax system, based on the founding principle that people react when they're taxed. This is only sometimes the intention of taxation, such as the tax on tobacco – so that people smoke less. Most taxes, however, change behaviour unintentionally. After all, it is not the lawmakers' intention that people should work less (or work cash in hand) *because* they are taxed, but that is precisely how some react. Nor is it desirable that businesses should move their headquarters abroad to save on tax. Vickrey asked himself: what could be taxed that can't migrate abroad, doesn't decrease, and which nobody can hide from the tax authorities? Land. Vickrey was in favour of abolishing most taxes altogether and replacing them with a land value tax. This had been suggested before in the economic bestseller of the nineteenth century, *Progress and Poverty* by Henry George, after whom the reforming idea was named. A good topic for Vickrey's Nobel Prize speech nonetheless.

Or should he talk about government debt? Vickrey was convinced that balancing the budget was a completely nonsensical aim that inevitably led to unemployment, which could have otherwise be avoided. It wasn't a burden on future generations, he thought, if the state borrowed money to invest. On the contrary, what would have happened if AT&T, private developers, and General Motors had been forced to 'balance their budgets' without any debts? Today we'd have a worse telephone network, fewer houses, and fewer cars. (Vickrey certainly didn't regard cars as the most indispensable of all consumer goods, but he could safely assume that the example would impress his readers.)

It's not only future generations that benefit if the state invests. Savers too rely on government debt. The period of time we live as pensioners became considerably longer in the twentieth century. More and more people want to save or have to save, because the state pension isn't sufficient to meet their needs. What some save, however, others must borrow. No bank in the world can afford to leave money untouched. But whereas the desire to save is becoming greater, businesses don't need to borrow as much money. Developed countries no longer have so much heavy industry, i.e. businesses needing to make huge investments in machinery at the outset. Small companies that provide services are becoming increasingly important, and these have a far lower capital requirement.

Savers offering more capital than the market needs isn't a sustainable state of affairs. Economic textbooks suggest a simple market solution: lower interest rates, which make saving less attractive but money cheaper to borrow. This results in fewer savings and more borrowers. At some point the supply and demand of savings capital are back in equilibrium.

If people are saving for retirement, however, this no longer works. According to Vickrey, anyone wanting to top up their pension to a particular level in old age needs to save more to achieve their goal when interest rates are falling. Not less, as the textbooks suggest. What to do, then, with the glut of savings?

In his speech Vickrey wouldn't have minced his words. A government that insists on following the ideology of the balanced budget will lead the country into recession. Perhaps he would have formulated it more polemically; after all, when referring to the automobile in America in an academic publication, he'd succeeded in smuggling in the expression 'rubber-tired sacred cow'. But three days after the announcement of the Nobel Prize and two months before the award ceremony in Stockholm, William Vickrey died. He suffered a heart attack at the wheel of his car.

12

Coase and the Economic Problems of Eternal Life

RONALD H. COASE

1910–2013

For many centuries, the notion of human beings achieving immortality was nothing more than a grotesque idea. In Greek mythology we find the story of Eos, goddess of the dawn, who couldn't cope with the death of beloved mortals: King Memnon, for example – her son by Prince Tithonus – who was slain by Achilles and who she cries over to this day (what we call the morning dew are in fact the tears of Eos). Not wishing to suffer the death of Memnon's father as well, the goddess begged Zeus to make him immortal. And so Tithonus aged without dying; he kept growing older, shrivelling miserably and losing all his strength. Eventually, nothing remained of his voice save for a shrill babble, and so some ancient writers had him turn into a cricket or a cicada.

This may have inspired Jonathan Swift, who has Gulliver visit the Luggnaggians, some of whom – very rarely, fortunately – are born immortal, known as Struldbruggs. When they reach the age of eighty, their misfortune is revealed; they have 'not only all the follies and infirmities of other old men'; they also become 'opinionative, peevish, covetous, morose, vain [and] talkative'. Their hair and teeth fall out, they lose all pleasure in eating and drinking, as well as in reading, because their memories are no longer sharp enough to remember the beginning of a sentence when they've got to the end.

Aging is a similarly unpleasant process in José Saramago's bleak and absurd novel *Death with Interruptions*. People become older and sicker, but they no longer die because Death has stopped working, at least in the unnamed country where the novel takes place. People soon come up with the idea of taking their bedridden relatives over the border, because in the neighbouring country death still occurs normally.

More desirable, at first glance at least, is the state of eternal youth that Raimondo Fosca achieves in Simone de Beauvoir's novel *All Men Are Mortal*, after drinking a magic elixir. As the novel arrives at the twentieth century, Fosca reaches 600 years of age, and is fated to go on like this forever, as he demonstrates by cutting his own throat. He has lived through several centuries and tried out many roles. His immortality makes him incredibly attractive to Regine, a stage actress, who likes the idea that someone will still be thinking of her in 10,000 years' time. Fosca, however, faces the unending horror of being the only person on the planet when all life has been extinguished – or almost all life, for there is an immortal white mouse who drank the elixir too – whereas people smarter than Fosca left it alone.

While we can be confident nobody will ever share the fate of Raimondo Fosca, there are a number of laboratories around the world investigating one dimension of his immortality: how to halt the process of aging.

As we age, to begin with our bodies can replace the dying cells. But as we get progressively older, the chromosomes become slightly shorter, and at some point we lose cells without any substitution. Ciliates, however, are protozoans that can keep dividing forever. And a few years ago we discovered the reason why: the enzyme telomerase rebuilds the ends of the chromosomes. For other sorts of damage to body cells, different solutions would be needed – perhaps tiny, helpful nano robots. Or we might finally understand the trick of the Greenland shark, which can live to over 400 years. Even experts can't tell apart the organs of a 100-year-old turtle from those of a ten-year-old one. The green hydra (a freshwater polyp) doesn't die of old age; the list of creatures that resist aging goes on and on.

If we were like these creatures we would be the exact opposite of Tithonus: we would stay young, but remain mortal. The current probability of a twenty-year-old dying within a year is about 0.05%. If they stay as healthy as they were at twenty, life expectancy rises to 2,000 years (and half of people would live to at least 1,386). What this would mean for population numbers is not readily clear. If everyone, as they do now, were to have on average two children around four to five decades before the end of their lives, nothing dramatic would occur. People would on average be older, even if they didn't look it, and there would be fewer births per year than now because it would take longer before people were sufficiently mature to have them.

This optimistic scenario is highly unlikely, however; after all, we don't know how old we would get, especially not if accidents are the most significant cause of death. And even if we did know, why would we want to wait so long before having children? Surely we'd want to meet our great-great-great-grandchildren. Besides, there's no reason to have only two children with a life expectancy of 2,000 years. Even having ten or twenty children would leave plenty of time for both parents to forge their careers. In short, demographic prognoses for the post-aging era are terribly difficult to arrive at, but one thing is certain: there would be too many people.

The first person to discover a cure for aging will face their wonder drug being rapidly outlawed, unless they also find a solution to the problem of overpopulation. Maybe there are people already working on this, who knows? And who might the successful pharmaceutical firm engage as a troubleshooter? Surely an economist – that is to say, an expert in dealing with scant resources. And which economist? Ronald Coase would have put himself forward. For economists in the twentieth and twenty-first centuries, immortality has represented a new, unusual problem, and Coase was one of the most original thinkers amongst the Nobel Prize winners in Economics. His famous theorem could also be applied to the problem of overpopulation.

Coase owed his career as an economist to a certain lack of

education. He at first wanted to study history, but his Latin wasn't good enough. His second choice would have been chemistry, but he was put off by the level of maths that was required. This is no secret; Coase includes it in the biographical sketch expected of every Nobel laureate in Economics. Like almost all of his predecessors and successors, Coase also says something personal about his parents. We learn, for example, that his father was a telegraphist with the post office, enjoyed playing a variety of sports, and even made the local bowls team, as well as writing for *Bowls News*. It's touching to see how one prize winner after another ensures their memories of their parents are immortalised in the annals of the Nobel Prize.

While still a student at the London School of Economics, Coase wrote his first research paper, which addressed a question that at first glance seems surprising: why do companies actually exist? Companies are organisations in which there is no negotiation over what is to be done and how – this is decided by the boss or department head. And yet outside of companies there are prices and markets we rely on and which for the most part work well. In a free-market economy nobody has to plan and order how much wheat, how many bikes, and how many books must be produced. Nonetheless almost exactly the amount of wheat, bikes, and books are produced as are wanted. And let's say, for example, the demand rises slightly for chia seeds, because that's the latest food trend. In that case, rising prices will signal to producers that it's worth producing more of them. Prices have an impact on the labour market too: many young people study law, not because they find it especially interesting, but because it can earn them money. If philosophers were better paid more people would study philosophy. Nobody needs to stipulate how many students should enrol for law and how many for philosophy.

Companies, on the other hand, are pockets of the planned economy. Within a company people don't follow the signals of market prices but the orders of their superiors. And the production manager can't choose on a daily basis which technology to select for manufacture because the machinery is already there and needs to be used. Isn't that inefficient?

A good example of production without companies is the film industry. The film producer owns nothing, not even a camera, and nor do they have any employees, save perhaps for an office assistant. Everything needed for a film is hired: lighting, technology, animal trainers, catering, make-up, costumes, stunt men – everything. When the film is finished everyone has fulfilled their contract with the producer and they all go their own way. But this is atypical, and Coase demonstrates why it wouldn't work in many sectors: using markets is simply too expensive for certain products and activities, and complicated contracts would have to be negotiated to cover all eventualities. The significance of this essay remained unrecognised for many years, but since then it has developed into a whole new field of research: 'new institutional economics'. This sets out to explain not only why companies exist, but also how best they can thrive; for example, by examining the question of whether a company should 'make or buy' – should something needed for production be bought from suppliers or made within the company itself?

Whatever industrial businesses manufacture themselves, one thing they don't produce in-house are the raw materials, which are bought in. Coase made use of this fact when he worked in one of the offices of Churchill's war cabinet in the Second World War, estimating how many tanks and aircrafts were being manufactured in Germany. While these figures themselves were kept secret, the production capacity and imports of important raw materials such as coal, steel, and copper into Germany were known. Churchill was so pleased with the conclusions Coase drew that he gave him another job: checking the production statistics of domestic industry. Churchill mistrusted British arms manufacturers – rightly so, as it would transpire.

The study that later made Coase famous overnight has a strange backstory. In 1959, when Coase was a professor at the University of Virginia, he published a paper on the allocation of frequencies to radio and television broadcasters. He insisted that frequencies should be treated like any other goods. Whereas most economists had little objection to this, they found one of his claims odd. Coase said the order in which broadcasters were allocated frequencies didn't matter: the end result would be efficient.

A group of economists from Chicago invited Coase to discuss his analysis. Before the start of the debate, a formal vote was taken in which twenty economists deemed Coase's arguments as flawed. One thought he was right: Coase himself. At the end of the debate Coase had all twenty-one votes. The defeated economists encouraged Coase to develop his ideas on frequencies at greater length, and the result was his famous article, 'The Problem of Social Cost'.

'Social costs' are the costs of production or consumption that are not borne by the actor that gives rise to them. If, for example, a factory releases effluent into a river, causing fish to die, there is a cost to society in the form of fewer edible fish. This cost is not incurred by the business, but by the people fishing – who catch fewer fish – or those who eat the fish and fall sick as a result. For a long time economists thought that such activities ought to be regulated or taxed to reduce them to an efficient level. Coase wasn't convinced by this. He collected cases of social costs that had been heard in court and worked out an argument for each of them.

One example was the case of Sturges v. Bridgman. The noise from a confectioner's machinery was severely hampering the work of a neighbouring doctor, Sturges. Amongst other things, he was unable to listen to his patients' chests when the machines were operating. This was back in 1879, which explains the lack of noise protection. The court upheld the doctor's case, deciding that he 'had the right to prevent the confectioner from using his machinery', as Coase put it, which wasn't synonymous with an outright ban on using the machinery.

For example, the following could have happened. The two parties could have negotiated the doctor's granting of an 'operating licence', by which the doctor renounced his rights (or assigned them to the confectioner) if the compensation offered by the confectioner was greater than the doctor's loss of income. How much the confectioner offered would depend on how much he earned through using his machinery. Ultimately he would continue to use it if it earned him more than it cost the doctor.

Now let's imagine the court hadn't found in favour of the doctor, but granted the confectioner the right to continue using his machinery. The doctor and confectioner could have negotiated here too; in this case, the compensation the doctor would have to pay the confectioner for not using his machinery. The result is the same: in the end the confectioner would continue using his machinery if it earned him more than it cost the doctor.

This means that the use of the machinery is not dependent on who the court judges to be in the right. Another example Coase gives is the case of a farmer whose herd of cattle damages a neighbouring farmer's wheat field (it's irrelevant whether or not the herd is permitted to continue using the wheat field; what matters is what the two farmers negotiate). Or the train that sparks, potentially causing fires along the tracks. The result is always the same: if rights without obstacles are negotiable it doesn't matter who is granted them in the first instance, for ultimately they will go to whoever ought to have them from an economic perspective. (Nowadays this is called the 'Coase Theorem', even though Coase himself never spoke of a theorem.)

Could negotiable rights also be used to prevent the over-population of our planet? It's impossible to imagine direct negotiations between perpetrators and victims in this scenario, but this isn't necessary. Anyone who wishes to have children would have to purchase some sort of licence, and there would be a limited number of licences, so that the earth could support humanity sustainably. If the Coase Theorem is applied to this case, it doesn't matter how the state distributes the licences. They could, for example, be drawn by lots; the important thing is that the licences can be sold on.

This sounds appalling, and it doesn't get any better when you flesh out the details. In Dmitry Glukhovsky's dystopian novel *Futu.re* the protagonist starts out as a member of a squad that tracks down people who are immortal but have children. The children remain alive, but the parents are given an injection that ages them rapidly and also renders them infertile. In Glukhovsky's world the European solution is that everyone has a right to immortality but not to have children, whereas the pan-American system works differently: the number of immortals is fixed, and if one of them dies because of an accident or suicide the medical treatment that gives immortality is auctioned to the highest bidder amongst mortals.

All this is still science fiction, even if some old people give the impression of having resisted the process of aging. Coase was one of these (maybe we could fantasise that this was his adviser's fee for our fictitious pharmaceutical firm).

Every year since 1992 – the year after Coase was awarded the Nobel Prize – the University of Chicago has invited an important economist to give a Coase Lecture in honour of Ronald Coase. In 2003 Coase himself was asked to deliver the lecture. He used the opportunity to express his surprise that he was giving a Coase Lecture, as this was what he'd been doing all his life. He thought it particularly awkward that the purpose of the event was to honour Ronald Coase; his mother and father ought to be the ones honoured rather than himself. In any case, for most people such tribute was superfluous – as Adam Smith pointed out, it's hard to find someone lacking in self-love.

At the time of this jaunty lecture Coase was ninety-two, but looked around twenty years younger. Afterwards, however, age caught up with him too. He lost his upright posture, his voice became feebler, and his mind strayed back to the topics he'd researched in his youth. A 2006 paper of his examined why General Motors had bought Fisher Body eighty years earlier, which till then had been its independent bodywork supplier. When Coase was ninety-eight, as a precaution the organisers of a conference recorded his talk so they could cut out pauses here or there. On 2 September 2013 Coase died at the age of one hundred and two. We will have to answer without him the question of how to deal with radically extended life expectancy, and soon, otherwise one day we'll wake up in a spinechilling novel.

13

Variations on Themes by Friedrich List

HENRI DE SAINT-SIMON, 1760–1825
ALEXANDER HAMILTON, 1755?–1804
ELIZABETH BOODY SCHUMPETER, 1898–1953
KARL MARX, 1818–1883
ROSA LUXEMBURG, 1871–1919

Friedrich List wasn't the first economist to think of shooting himself. The Frenchman Henri de Saint-Simon tried this in 1823, but it only cost him an eye. Saint-Simon was one of the 'early socialists' who Marx and Engels had a low opinion of: poor at analysis, only good at sketching utopias. Like List, Saint-Simon was not lacking in confidence in his early years; as a seventeen-year-old he ordered his valet to wake him up every morning with the words, 'Get up, my Lord, you have great things to achieve.' The title of count, which Saint-Simon relinquished after the French Revolution, was real, whereas his descent from Charlemagne was made up. Like List, Saint-Simon tried his hand as a publisher and journalist after many other different ventures. One of his periodicals, *L'Organisateur*, contained his famous 'parable', in which Saint-Simon begins by describing the misery that would ensue if the 3,000 most capable scientists, artists, and workers suddenly died. He lists forty professional groups in detail, from physicists and chemists, writers and sculptors, to engineers, doctors, clockmakers, miners, cloth manufacturers, printers, and farriers. Such a calamity would turn France into a body without a soul and throw the country back at least a generation in competition with other nations.

What would happen, by contrast, if instead of these 3,000 useful people, it was the 30,000 people at the top of the state who died? Some Saint-Simon mentions by name, beginning with the brother of the king, then the dukes of Angoulême, Berry, Orléand, and Bourbon, followed by ministers of state, officials dealing with petitions in the council of state, cardinals, prefects, judges, large landowners, and so on. This would be a sad calamity but it wouldn't be harmful to the state. The reason is not that it's easy to step into the shoes of a duke or large landowner and take on their duties. No, it's because these people don't do anything productive and only cause damage by attracting money and recognition that ought to go to the scientists, artists, craftsmen, and other professions.

The upcoming bourgeoisie liked this; after all, Saint-Simon was calling for a government of the most talented and productive, which according to him wouldn't include the nobility, but definitely the entrepreneurs. Somewhat naively he believed for a while that what was good for the entrepreneurs was also good for the workers. It's no wonder that his publications were supported by wealthy citizens, until all of a sudden this source dried up. One of the noblemen who Saint-Simon had named, the Duke de Berry, was stabbed to death. The murderer had acted alone but had he been incited to kill by Saint-Simon's parable? Saint-Simon was charged, which didn't lead to a conviction but financially put him in a right pickle.

After his failed suicide attempt Saint-Simon had another two years to live. Improving the lot of the poor was still a subject close to his heart, but he no longer backed the entrepreneurs' pursuit of profit, advocating instead something more fundamental: a new Christianity (his last book was entitled *Le Nouveau Christianisme*). He left behind the 'Saint-Simonists', a sect with all the trimmings. Clashes occurred between sect leaders over monogamy versus promiscuity, leading to schism and then the end of the sect after a few years, with just enough time for some List-like worldly endeavours, including an initiative to build the French railway network.

Another economist whom Death granted a reprieve, if only for a day, was Alexander Hamilton, List's forerunner as an advocate of infant-industry tariffs. In his *Report on Manufactures*, which he presented to Congress in 1791, he put forward his arguments for the protection of young industries. Although Hamilton's concrete suggestions were initially rejected, his work created a favourable atmosphere for imposing tariffs. In 1795 Hamilton's tenure as the first US secretary of the treasury came to an end. He returned to jobs he'd done before, working as a lawyer, then in the military. As a friend of, and adviser to, George Washington he still tried to influence politics. One of those he made an enemy of during this period was Aaron Burr, who was vice president under Thomas Jefferson when he challenged Hamilton to a duel.

Burr's bullet destroyed parts of Hamilton's lungs and liver, and damaged the spinal cord; he was immediately paralysed and knew he wouldn't survive the other injuries. He had thirty-one hours left to say goodbye to his wife, children, and twenty friends. He left us with the question: what would you say if you knew this was your last day? And why didn't you say it earlier?

Schumpeter thought highly of both Hamilton and List. As for List's 'best-known contribution to the education of German public opinion on economic policy, the infant-industry argument, this is clearly Hamiltonian and part of the economic wisdom that List imbibed during his stay in the United States,' he wrote. He first warned people not to over-estimate List's analytical skills, before heaping effusive praise on him: 'He was a great patriot, a brilliant journalist with defi-nite purpose, and an able economist who co-ordinated well whatever seemed useful for implementing his vision. Is this not enough?'

So Schumpeter wrote in his *History of Economic Analysis*. This is a book that runs to 1,500 pages, a demonstration of

Schumpeter's vast erudition, brimming with forceful judgements, but also on a par with Joyce's *Ulysses* or Musil's *The Man without Qualities*: a masterpiece that has to be religiously admired, even though very few people can claim to have actually read it.

Schumpeter died without having finished this work. We have his third wife, Elizabeth Boody Schumpeter, to thank for the fact that his manuscripts were turned into a book. In 1934 he was the second referee on her dissertation about English foreign trade, and by 1935 they were a couple in Harvard; after some hesitation, Schumpeter brought himself to marry for the third time in 1937.

At the time Elizabeth was researching the Japanese economy. She warned against underestimating Japanese economic strength, and she didn't believe that economic sanctions were a suitable way to end the war that Japan was waging against China. The Japanese could produce weapons and munitions anyway, while sanctions weakened the position of the many Japanese who desired a more liberal government and less aggressive foreign policy. In 1940 she also predicted Japan's non-aggression pact with the Soviet Union of the following year.

There weren't many genuine Japan experts in the US. After the Japanese attack on Pearl Harbour in December 1941 the government could have taken her on as an adviser. But the FBI regarded her as suspect: Bureau chief J. Edgar Hoover thought her publications were paid Japanese propaganda that contravened the espionage law. He was unsatisfied with the results of his agents who interrogated not only Elizabeth but also neighbours, friends, and colleagues of the Schumpeters. The questioning brought up nothing that Hoover could use – Joseph Schumpeter was a committed anti-Nazi, whereas Elizabeth had begun researching Japan in 1934, long before the war could be predicted, and what she published allowed no clear conclusions. Hoover thought that the next agent who interrogated Elizabeth ought to do more homework on the case. And indeed, it was discovered that in the late 1930s a large sum of money had suddenly appeared in her account: who was that from? The answer was simple: the suspect had sold a house. No charges were brought.

Besides her own research, Elizabeth did as much as she could to support her husband, who was plunged into depression by the Second World War, and suffered from self-doubt and mood swings, which he hid behind his charm. She put up with the fact that he still kept a photo of Annie, his second wife, on his bedside table, and helped him work on his *History of Economic Analysis*, his weighty last work, about which she said, 'Since we cannot have a child, let's have this book together.'

When Elizabeth was diagnosed with breast cancer in 1948 Schumpeter was distraught and confided to his diary his belief that Elizabeth had given more to him than she'd received back. It would remain that way. A mastectomy and radiotherapy gave her a reprieve. She outlived Schumpeter by three years, during which she devoted herself to the task of putting together the manuscript fragments that were in various libraries, studies, and an attic room, some handwritten, some already typed. She had to edit and make decisions, for example, about undated alternative versions of certain passages and missing titles. She was still busy with this task in the last weeks of her life; terminally ill, she worked on the indexes. Like Schumpeter, she wasn't alive to see the book's publication.

If there's one posthumous work on economics which is more famous than Schumpeter's, it's volume two of *Das Kapital*. In my chapter on List there was just enough space to mention that Marx owed his editorial position at the *Rheinische Zeitung* to List's tumble from his horse, which was probably the only reason he met the wealthy Friedrich Engels, without whose support he would have barely left anything still remembered today. Instead he was able to burden Engels with the completion of volumes two and three of *Das Kapital* – and this was one hell of a burden.

Marx had even kept putting off the first volume. In 1845 Engels wrote to him: 'Make sure you finish your book on economics.' In 1851 Marx said he needed another five weeks to be done with 'all the economic crap'. In 1859 a preparatory work appeared, and finally the first volume of *Das Kapital* was published in 1867. For the two subsequent volumes he left behind substantial manuscripts, totalling more than 1,600 pages, but all very fragmentary and in tiny, indecipherable handwriting. Writing wasn't his problem – knowing when to stop was. In a questionnaire his daughter Jenny gave him, he put under 'Motto': *De omnibus dubitandum*, 'everything must be doubted'. He devoted the last decade of his life to procrastination, learning Russian and pursuing studies in such areas as ethnology, physiology, chemistry, and geology.

Engels was an efficient author with a neat desk in a very tidy study. He was the total opposite of Marx, who knew that Engels would be able to do something with his manuscripts. And thus it came to pass: in 1885 Engels published the second volume, and in 1894 the third. Marx must have thought it pretty likely that he'd die before Engels. Since the age of forty-five he'd been plagued by chronic boils and carbuncles, wrongly treated with arsenic. In his letters to Engels he goes into great detail about the 'filthy carbuncles' or the 'dog of a carbuncle' or the 'monster carbuncle'. He also suffered from smoker's bronchitis and liver trouble, and complained about 'bilious conditions' and sleeplessness. Today his probable cause of death is reckoned to have been pulmonary tuberculosis, maybe lung cancer too.

The theory that Marx left behind in manuscript form wasn't fully thought through; in many places Engels is cited by the publisher and editor as co-author. This is true, for example, of the crisis and collapse theory, one of the best-known sections in these two volumes. This posits that sooner or later the larger and better-funded businesses will eliminate the smaller ones until they themselves are ousted. What's left at the end of this process are a few especially crisis-prone businesses with ever lower profit rates, as well as an army of workers who nobody needs anymore.

The 'law of the tendential fall in the rate of profit' remains a controversial subject, both empirically and theoretically, across all camps of economic research. On Marx's side we find liberal-conservative economists such as Hans-Werner Sinn, while we've already discussed the criticism from the pen of the Marx's admirer Schumpeter. But genuine Marxists criticise Marx too, such as Yanis Varoufakis, the telegenic, motorbike-riding economist-professor and Greek finance minister for almost half a year during the climax of the EU's 2015 financial and economic crisis, of which his country was at the very centre. He criticises Marx's attempt to gain insight into capitalism from a deterministic mathematical model. Varoufakis is right: mathematical models form the core of *Das Kapital*, which doesn't mean that the words around them are unimportant, not least because they humour the reader with pearls such as: 'Capital is dead labour that only lives by sucking living labour, like a vampire, and the more it sucks out, the more it keeps living.' But what Marx overlooks, according to Varoufakis, is a key reason for capitalist dynamism: that very part of human labour which is unquantifiable. Marx ought to have seen, he says, that his 'laws' were not unchangeable.

Rosa Luxemburg too had her doubts about the law of the tendential fall in the rate of profit. She wrote, 'The collapse of capitalism from the fall in the rate of profit has a long way to go yet, roughly until the sun burns out.'

And because we have now mentioned her name, we ought to tell Rosa Luxemburg's story as well. At the age of sixteen she passed her school leaving exams in Warsaw. She got brilliant grades, but in Poland – like most other countries – women were not allowed to study. In any case she would have soon been arrested for socialist agitation. The country she could flee to and also study in was Switzerland. At the University of Zurich she enrolled for all the subjects she could before specialising in economic theory, in which she gained her PhD in 1897, when she'd just turned twenty-six. It says a lot about Rosa Luxemburg that she chose as her supervisor Julius Wolf, a bourgeois economist and harsh critic of Marx. He awarded Rosa Luxemburg's thesis on *The Industrial Development of Poland* the distinction of magna cum laude, but criticised her for occasionally using 'expressions from socialist pamphlets'.

In addition to her substantial journalistic and political activity she would go on to write more books on economic issues. Published in 1913 was *The Accumulation of Capital: A Contribution to an Economic Explanation of Imperialism*, and posthumously her incomplete *Introduction to Economic Theory* appeared, which was mostly based on her lectures to the SPD's national academy. These works have largely been forgotten, and if there is something of Rosa Luxemburg's still worth reading today, it's not her economic writings but her wonderful letters from prison.

She was given her first custodial sentence in 1904: three months imprisonment for lèse-majesté, having allegedly said about Wilhelm II, 'The man who talks of the decent, secure existence of the German workers has no clue about facts.'

There were further short spells in prison, but things got really unpleasant in 1913. Even the SPD, of which Rosa Luxemburg was still a member at the time, agreed to greater military expenditure. She was horrified and tried to counter the emerging enthusiasm for the war: 'If we are asked to raise our murderous weapons against our brothers in France or any other country, we will say, "No, we refuse."' The public prosecutor regarded this as incitement to disobey the law and directives of the government. She spent more than three years during the First World War in prison. In February 1917 she wrote from Wronke (now Wronki) fortress:

Let there be only two syllables on my gravestone: 'chee-chee'. Because that's the song of the great tit which I can mimic so well that the birds come running to me immediately. And just think that in this chee-chee, which usually is so clear and thin, glinting like a steel needle, I have heard for the past two days a faint trill, a tiny sound from the chest. Do you know, Fräulein Jacob, what this means? It is the first stirring of the coming spring. In spite of the snow and frost and loneliness, we – the great tit and I, believe in the coming spring! And if, out of impatience, I fail to experience it, do not forget that on my gravestone there must be nothing save for 'chee-chee'.

On 8 November 1918, with the war as good as over, she was released. On 15 January 1919 a far-right army officer, who rode roughshod over the law to prevent the formation of a soviet republic in Germany, ordered her murder. Her body was thrown into Berlin's Landwehr Canal. We don't know what happened to her after that. The badly decayed body that was found on 31 May at Freiarchen Bridge could have been Rosa Luxemburg or not. (Bodies in the water weren't uncommon – 400 m separated the spot where Rosa Luxemburg was thrown in and where the body was found. In this stretch of water in February 1919 a diver found two female corpses and a male one, along with seventy rifles.) The autopsy report from 1919 is not convincing at any rate. A few years back a Berlin coroner made headlines with his hypothesis that a body found in the water, which had been in the basement of La Charité hospital for decades, could be that of Rosa Luxemburg. But this seems pretty doubtful; all attempts to find traces of Rosa Luxemburg's DNA have failed.

Nothing remains of her grave in Friedrichsfelde Central Cemetery; it was flattened in 1941. What really happened to her dead body in 1919 will remain the secret of the great tits, whose chee-chee nobody understands anymore.

Notes and Sources

On the **foreword**: The difference in life expectancy between authors and other artists isn't just a trifle. In David Kaun's random sample (1991) he found that authors died on average at 61.7 years of age, while other artists lived from six to ten years longer, beginning with cartoonists (67.9), via musicians, architects, painters, composers, singers, and dancers to the longest-lived artists of them all: photographers and directors (both averaging at 72). Little comfort is offered by the study carried out in 1994 by the psychiatrist Felix Post into the psychopathology of various professions. His survey found symptoms of severe psychological disorder in 46 per cent of writers, but only in 17 to 18 per cent of academics and politicians. And his colleague Professor Donald W. Goodwin (1998) stated that only one profession – barkeepers – suffered more often from cirrhosis of the liver than writers.

In the epigraph, the Enzenberger quote is drawn from a conversation with Alexander Kluge (http://kluge.library.cornell. edu/de/conversations/enzensberger/film/1970/transcript); the quote by Roland Barthes can be found in Ribière (2011).

The essay cited on **Cantillon** by W. Stanley Jevons (entitled *Richard Cantillon and the Nationality of Political Economy*) is easily available in a number of reprints, including as an appendix to the English (re?)translation by Henry Higgs. There is scant evidence for the reports that Cantillon's book was already circulating as a manuscript many years before his death. What has been found out about Cantillon's life since Jevons, Jevons himself would surely have unearthed in his research if it hadn't come to an abrupt end: on 13 August 1882 Jevons drowned while swimming on the south coast of England. And so the authoritative biography didn't appear until a century later (Murphy, 1986). I'd like to thank Harald Hagemann for pointing me to Cantillon.

Bentham wrote between ten and fifteen pages a day; much of it is still unpublished, but even the tomes that have made it into print are enough to exasperate the reader. Anybody wishing to embark on reading Bentham should definitely start with his main work, *An Introduction to the Principles of Morals and Legislation* (1780).

Stark (1941) gives a good overview of Bentham's economic writings. For medical literature on Bentham: see Lucas and Sheeran (2006) on signs of Asperger syndrome in Bentham, and Lewenz and Pearson (1904) on his head.

The fact that Bentham made available his oven for experiments with mummification doesn't mean that there is verified information on the carrying out of such experiments; see

Marmoy (1958). The experiments referred to are: Knetsch and Sinden (1984); Kahneman, Knetsch, and Thaler (1990).

Although Bentham must have made a huge effort explaining the new ideas of diminishing marginal utility, he wasn't the first to come up with the idea. This honour (according to Kauder, 1965, Chapter III) goes to Daniel Bernoulli. Bentham 'rediscovered' the idea, however, without being familiar with Bernoulli's work.

The phrase 'Bentham's arguments for giving women the franchise' shouldn't hide the fact that he wasn't absolutely certain on this point in all his writings; he also advanced counter-arguments such as women's supposed lack of rationality and their tendency towards superstition. See Ball (1980); Campos Boralevi (1980).

The Kufstein regional court protocol on the post-mortem findings has been taken from Volume VIII of Friedrich **List's** works (Berlin: 1933, p. 846) – word for word, but without indicating abbreviations. In the same volume (p. 122) is his aforementioned request for permission to marry, from 1 February 1818, which for fans of language evolution is reproduced here word for word:

His Royal Majesty
I beg ... for permission to be able to marry Karoline Neidhard, née Seybold, and furthermore:

1. for the most gracious dispensation from the threefold reading of the banns
2. for the most gracious permission to be united in Wertheim, Baden, where my bride is currently resident

With the deepest reverence
His Royal Majesty's
most humble, faithful and obedient servant
Professor List.

A good biography of List in English is by Henderson (1983), while the exhibition catalogue *Friedrich List und seine Zeit* ('Friedrich List and his time', 1989) is rather beautiful.

Thünen's worries about Hermann were totally unjustified; both sons became competent farmers (Hippauf, 2000). Thünen's profit-share model also continued until Tellow was sold by the last owner in the family, his grandson Alexander, and only then rescinded by the latter's successor in 1896 (Vonderach, 2004; the entire chapter on Thünen and his estate is worth a read). The house is still standing and nowadays it is home to the Thünen Museum, which in 2013 put together a book-sized collection of quotes from Thünen's works and letters, as if he were some kind of Mecklenburg Dalai Lama. You can get a more realistic picture of the everyday man ('Dear Son – I came back from Güstrow yesterday and I am hastening to send you news by tomorrow's post about the wool market and my wool sales...') from the comprehensive edition of Thünen's letters, which was published by Metropolis-Verlag in 2011. My quotations have been taken from this and *The Isolated State*. His youthful piece about Gross Flottbek appears in Rieter (1995).

Samuelson (1983, p. 1486) points out that the market wage can be higher than Thünen's natural wage.

For Alexander Vasilievich **Chayanov**, see Bourgholtzer (1999) and Janssen (2010). The complete plea for clemency exists only in the Russian source, from which Schulze (2001) has translated excerpts of the interrogation protocol and other documents. The print edition of the novel (Chayanov, 1981) has the advantage over the online edition in that it contains a foreword by a Soviet functionary which is enlightening about the – as he sees it – reactionary character of the novel in its 1920 edition. The major academic work is Chayanov (1966). The quote about pressing the ox into the form of a camel is taken from Bogomasow and Drosdowa (1999, p. 58).

Hayek's comment about **Keynes** is from an interview that Leo Rosten did with him in 1978. You can find it on YouTube by searching for 'Hayek on Keynes's Ignorance of Economics'. The Asquith anecdote is from Holroyd (1995); the letter to Churchill and his reply can be found in Keynes (1981, p. 749f.). On Keynes's relationship to Lytton Strachey see Davenport-Hines (2015, Chapter 5) and for the banana parable see Barens (1989). I've taken the information about Keynes's final lecture from Skidelsky (2004, p. 832). That Keynes in his dying words referred to 'A Night-Piece on Death' (rather than any other of Parnell's poems) is a reasonable hunch, but admittedly no more than that. Uwe Gressmann's poem 'Todeserwartung', from which I quoted at the end of this chapter with the kind permission of the Akademie der Künste, can be found in *Schreibheft 83* (August 2014, p. 146).

The **Stackelberg** quotes are from no. 1, year 7 (1932) of *Jungnationale Stimmen* ('A biological consideration...' p. 4; 'Liberation of those sections...' p. 5) and vol. 4, no. 1 (1934) of *Westdeutscher Akademischer Rundschau* ('The researcher is free...' p. 5). Stackelberg's *Gesammelte wirtschaftswissenschaftliche Abhandlungen*, which were published in two volumes by Transfer-Verlag Regensburg in 1992, contain a comprehensive bibliography. This includes a biography by Hans Möller, a student of Stackelberg. (This book doesn't contain his report of how Stackelberg's 'exile' came about, for which I must thank Hans Nutzinger. On 23 October 1940 Hitler tried in vain in Hendaye to make Franco enter the war. To gloss over the failure of this meeting, a German–Spanish exchange of at least one academic was arranged. Because of his language skills Stackelberg was an obvious candidate and Möller advised him to take up the offer.)

The aforementioned size of **Schumpeter's** *Theory of Economic Development*, 550 pages, refers to the first edition, which the author later edited to make it considerably shorter and more readable (the comparison with the 'canals on Mars' is only in the first edition, however, along with 'real blokes' and 'thirst for action'). I found Ehrig and Staroske (2016) helpful for this chapter. The quotes from his diary were taken from Annette Schäfer's Schumpeter biography (2008).

An excellent collection of sources and texts by and about Schumpeter can be found at http://www.schumpeter.info. I'm very grateful to Mathias Erlei for his advice about Schumpeter's potential for a book like this.

The Sherlock Holmes story by Arthur Conan Doyle mentioned in the chapter on John **von Neumann** is 'The Final Problem', which was first published in the *Strand Magazine* in 1893. Oskar Morgenstern referred to it in his book *Wirtschaftsprognose* (Vienna: 1928). John von Neumann's essay 'Zur Theorie der Gesellschaftsspiele' was published in *Mathematische Annalen* 100 (1928, pp. 295–300).

Von Neumann was a Jew by birth, for which reason the young Oskar Morgenstern could have barely imagined working with him one day, nor that the two men would become friends. At the beginning of his career in Vienna he was a nasty anti-Semite; for example, as a student he wrote in his diary the following: 'Now I know why the Jews hate Fichte so much. It's because he said, "All Jews should have their heads chopped off one night." All great men back then were anti-Semites as only the great ones could recognise the danger that was lurking. Anybody who's not an anti-Semite now is criminal.'

Quoted in Rellstab (1992). Morgenstern himself was taken for a Jew, however, whether this was on account of his name or the round glasses sitting on a nose that the Viennese Nazis considered too Jewish. At any rate, it delayed his post-doctoral degree by a year. This and other instances of discrimination cured him completely of his anti-Semitism.

Emanuel Lasker's attempt at a poker analysis can be found in his book *Das verständige Kartenspiel* (Berlin: 1929).

From Heims (1980) I've taken, amongst other things, the anecdote about von Neumann's assumption that his mother must be doing a calculation in her head. Other good biographies are: Poundstone (1992), which contains a helpful, non-technical introduction into game theory and the quote about the Hungarians' dislike of Russia (p. 143); Israel and Millán Gasca (2009); Leonard (2010); and Macrae (1992). Von Neumann's position on the risks of atomic technology I have taken from Halmos (1973).

Frank (2003) has a detailed list of sources for **Schmölders**. Schmölders (1998) is the autobiography and Schmölders (1930) the study on prohibition. On German economists in exile cf. Hagemann (2005).

My source for **Vickrey's** experiment with wireless road pricing is the paper by Ron Harstad for the *Dictionary of Scientific Biology*, available online as a manuscript here: http://ideas. repec.org/p/umc/wpaper/0519.html.

Max B. Sawicky provides the Titanic quote as well as other memories of Vickrey (http://wealthandwant.com/auth/Vickrey.html).

The telephone conversation with Vickrey after he'd just won the Nobel Prize comes from Mason Gaffney: 'Warm Memories of Bill Vickrey' (http://wealthandwant.com/auth/Vickrey.html). On the Rip van Winkle Award and other biographical details, cf. the foreword by Jacques Drèze and Richard Arnott in Vickrey (1994).

The many economists who are surprised that Vickrey auctions existed before Vickrey should read the article by Lucking-Reiley (2000). Vickrey (1996) contains his recommendations on tax-policy reform; on his macro-economics cf. these two posthumous publications: Vickrey (1997) and Vickrey (1998).

A market for the right to have children as a way of combating overpopulation was first proposed by the deeply religious economist Kenneth E. Boulding (1964). Unfortunately he neglects to refer to any sources, and so we can only speculate that he was inspired by **Coase** (1959, 1960). Most economists talk of negative externalities rather than social costs, but Coase didn't like this term.

I'm unaware of any source that suggests List knew of **Saint-Simon's** abortive suicide attempt, but it is certainly possible. Four years before List's death Lorenz von Stein wrote about

Saint-Simon's suicide attempt in his book *Sozialismus und Kommunismus des heutigen Frankreichs*, claiming rather dramatically that 'nobody departs without having first completed his task'. Johann Heinrich von Thünen related these words to himself, citing them twice in his letters. Saint-Simon's parable (like the sentence the young Saint-Simon had himself woken up with) can be found in Ramm (ed., 1956), amongst others.

Alexander **Hamilton** is not the only economist to have been victim to a pistol duel. The same fate befell Ferdinand Lassalle (1825–1864). Although chiefly known as a politician (he was the first president of the *Allgemeiner Deutscher Arbeiterverein*, from which the SPD later emerged), his few economic writings were praised by Schumpeter as 'brilliant'. What became well known was Lassalle's 'iron wage law', which says that 'the average worker's wage always remains at the minimum subsistence level routinely required to keep living and procreate' – so long as circumstances don't change. Lassalle was approaching forty when he took up with the capricious daughter of the Bavarian envoy in Switzerland. Her family was not exactly thrilled about the Jewish workers' leader, who was almost twice the age of their daughter. Her father let his future son-in-law represent him in a duel. After being shot in the privates, Lassalle, who only a few years earlier had called duels 'an absurd fossil of a superseded stage of civilisation', lived three more days.

On Elizabeth **Boody Schumpeter** see McCraw (2008); the

quotation is on p. 519. An example of her Japan research is Boody Schumpeter (1939).

On Karl **Marx's** ailments see Gross (1983). For Engels's work on Volumes 2 and 3 of *Das Kapital* see Roth (2013). I've taken Varoufakis's criticism of Marx from Varoufakis (2015). Hans-Werner Sinn (2017) defends him against Rosa Luxemburg.

The coroner referred to in the Rosa **Luxemburg** section is Michael Tsokos (2009; a critical view of this can be found in Laschitza and Gietinger, 2010). I've quoted the letter from Luxemburg (1990, p. 326f.). In another lovely selection of her letters (Luxemburg, 1972) one can find the following quote – a fitting sentiment to round off a book on economic research, as pertinent today as it was in 1917:

> The more that wicked and awful things happen every day, unrestrained and excessive, the calmer and more convinced I become that one cannot apply a moral yardstick to an element – a buran [snowstorm], a flood or an eclipse of the sun – but view them merely as something given, an object of research and knowledge.

Bibliography

Ball, Terence (1980), 'Was Bentham a Feminist?', *The Bentham Newsletter*, 4, pp. 25–52.

Barens, Ingo (1989), 'From the "Banana Parable" to the Principle of Effective Demand: Some Reflections on the Origin, Development and Structure of Keynes' *General Theory*', in Donald A. Walker (ed.), *Perspectives on the History of Economic Thought, Volume II: Twentieth-Century Economic Thought* (Aldershot: Elgar) pp. 111–32.

Bogomasow, Gennady Y. and **Natalia P. Drosdowa** (1999), 'Alexander Wassiljewitsch Tschajanow: Leben und Werk', in Bertram Schefold (ed.), *Vademecum zu einem russischen Klassiker der Agrarökonomie* (Düsseldorf: Verlag Wirtschaft und Finanzen) pp. 37–74.

Boody Schumpeter, Elizabeth (1939), 'The Problem of Sanctions in the Far East', *Pacific Affairs*, 12, pp. 245–62.

Boulding, Kenneth E. (1964), *The Meaning of the Twentieth Century* (New York: Harper & Row).

Bourgholtzer, Frank (1999), *Aleksandr Chayanov and Russian Berlin* (London: Frank Cass).

Campos Boralevi, Lea (1980), 'In Defence of a Myth', The Bentham Newsletter, 4, pp. 33–46a.

Chayanov, Alexander V. (1920), 'The Journey of my Brother Alexei into the Land of Peasant Utopia', tandfonline.com/doi/abs/10.1080/03066157608438004.

Chayanov, Alexander V. (1966), 'Peasant Farm Organization', in D. Thorner, B. Kerblay and R.E.F. Smith (eds), *Chayanov: The Theory of Peasant Economy* (Homewood, Illinois: Irwin).

Coase, Ronald H. (1959), 'The Federal Communications Commission', *Journal of Law and Economics*, 2, pp. 1–40.

Coase, Ronald H. (1960), 'The Problem of Social Cost', *Journal of Law and Economics*, 3, pp. 1–44.

Davenport-Hines, Richard (2015), *Universal Man: The Seven Lives of John Maynard Keynes* (London: William Collins).

Ehrig, Detlev and **Uwe Staroske** (2016), 'Der Weltenherrscher ökonomischer Dynamik. Zum Schumpeterschen Unternehmerverständnis', in Harald Hagemann and Jürgen Kromphardt (eds), *Keynes, Schumpeter und die Zukunft der entwickelten kapitalistischen Volkswirtschaften* (Marburg: Metropolis) pp. 169–203.

Frank, Björn (2003), Günter Schmölders and the Economics of Prohibition, in Warren J. Samuels (ed.), *European Economists of the Early 20th Century, Vol. 2, Studies of Neglected Continental Thinkers of Germany and Italy* (Cheltenham: Edward Elgar) pp. 281–94.

Goodwin, Donald W. (1988), *Alcohol and the Writer* (Kansas City: Andrews & McMeel).

Gross, Gerhard (1983), 'Die Dummheit im Kopf und die Paralysis in den Gliedern', *Deutsches Ärzteblatt*, 80/10, pp. 104–11.

Hagemann, Harald (2005), 'Dismissal, Expulsion, and Emigration of German-Speaking Economists after 1933', *Journal of the History of Economic Thought*, 27, pp. 405–20.

Halmos, Paul R. (1973), 'The Legend of John von Neumann', *The American Mathematical Monthly*, 80/4, pp. 382–94.

Heims, Steve J. (1980), *John von Neumann and Norbert Wiener: From Mathematics to the Technologies of Life and Death* (Cambridge, MA: MIT Press).

Henderson, William O. (1983), *Friedrich List: Economist and Visionary* (London: Frank Cass).

Hippauf, Renate (2000), *Johann Heinrich von Thünen: ein Lebensbild* (Rostock: Hinstorff).

Holroyd, Michael (1995), *Lytton Strachey: The New Biography* (New York: Farrar, Strauss & Giroux).

Israel, Giorgio and Ana Millán Gasca (2009), *The World as a Mathematical Game: John von Neumann and Twentieth Century Science* (Basel: Birkhäuser).

Janssen, Hauke (2010), 'Alexander W. Tschajanow (1888–1937) und die russische Emigration in Deutschland', in Heinz D. Kurz (ed.), *Studien zur Entwicklung der ökonomischen Theorie XXIV: Wechselseitige Einflüsse zwischen dem deutschen wirtschaftswissenschaftlichen Denken und dem anderer europäische Sprachräume* (Berlin: Duncker & Humblot) pp. 119–39.

Kahneman, Daniel, Jack L. Knetsch and Richard H. Thaler (1990), 'Experimental Tests of the Endowment Effect and the Coase Theorem', *Journal of Political Economy*, 98, pp. 1325–48.

Kauder, Emil (1965), *A History of Marginal Utility* (Princeton, NJ: Princeton University Press).

Kaun, David E. (1991), 'Writers Die Young: The Impact of Work and Leisure on Longevity', *Journal of Economic Psychology*, 12, pp. 381–99.

Keynes, John Maynard (1981), *The Collected Writings of John Maynard Keynes, Vol. XIX: Activities 1922–1929* (London: Macmillan).

Knetsch, Jack L. and J.A. Sinden (1984), 'Willingness to Pay and Compensation Demanded: Experimental Evidence of an Unexpected Disparity in Measures of Value', *Quarterly Journal of Economics*, 99, pp. 507–21.

Laschitza, Annelies and Klaus Gietinger (eds, 2010), *Rosa Luxemburgs Tod. Dokumente und Kommentare* (Leipzig: Rosa-Luxemburg-Stiftung Sachsen).

Leonard, Robert J. (2010), *Von Neumann, Morgenstern, and the Creation of Game Theory: From Chess to Social Science, 1900–1960* (Cambridge: Cambridge University Press).

Lewenz, M.A. and Karl Pearson (1904), 'On the

Measurement of Internal Capacity from Cranial Circumferences', *Biometrika*, 3, pp. 366–97.

Lucas, Philip and **Anne Sheeran** (2006), 'Asperger's Syndrome and the Eccentricity and Genius of Jeremy Bentham', *Journal of Bentham Studies*, 8, pp. 1–37.

Luxemburg, Rosa (1972), *Briefe aus dem Gefängnis*, 7th edition (Berlin: Dietz).

Luxemburg, Rosa (1990), *Herzlichst Ihre Rosa: Ausgewählte Briefe*, 2nd edition (Berlin: Dietz).

Macrae, Norman (1992), *John von Neumann: The Scientific Genius who Pioneered the Modern Computer, Game Theory, Nuclear Deterrence and Much More* (New York: Random House).

McCraw, Thomas K. (2010), *Prophet of Innovation: Joseph Schumpeter and Creative Destruction* (Cambridge, MA: Harvard University Press).

Marmoy, C.F.A (1958), 'The "Auto-Icon" of Jeremy Bentham at University College, London', *Medical History*, 2, pp. 77–88.

Murphy, Antoin E. (1986), *Richard Cantillon: Entrepreneur and Economist* (Oxford: Clarendon Press).

Post, Felix (1994), 'Creativity and Psychopathology: A Study of 291 World-Famous Men', *The British Journal of Psychiatry*, 165, pp. 22–34, cited in Dean Kenneth Simonton (2014), 'The Mad (Creative) Genius: What Do We Know after a Century of Historiometric Research?', in James C. Kaufman (ed.), *Creativity and Mental Illness* (Cambridge, Cambridge University Press) pp. 25–41.

Poundstone, William (1992), *Prisoner's Dilemma* (New York, London (et al.): Doubleday).

Ramm, Thilo (ed., 1956), *Der Frühsozialismus. Ausgewählte Quellentexte* (Stuttgart: Kröner).

Recktenwald, Horst C. (ed., 1971), *Geschichte der Politischen Ökonomie. Eine Einführung in Lebensbildern* (Stuttgart: Kröner).

Rellstab, Urs (1992), *Ökonomie und Spiele. Die Entstehungsgeschichte der Spieltheorie aus dem Blickwinkel des Ökonomen Oskar Morgenstern*, (Chur (et al.): Rüegger).

Ribière, Mireille (2011), 'Barthes – The Early Years', http://www.mireilleribiere.com/downloads/Roland-Barthes-The-Early-Years/BarthesEarlyYears1.Childhood.pdf.

Rieter, Heinz (ed., 1995), *Studien zur Entwicklung der ökonomischen Theorie XIV: Johann Heinrich von Thünen als Wirtschaftstheoretiker* (Berlin: Duncker & Humblot).

Roth, Regina (2013), *Die Herausgabe von Band 2 und 3 des Kapital durch Engels, Marx-Engels-Jahrbuch 2012–13* (Berlin: AkademieVerlag) pp. 168–82.

Samuelson, Paul A. (1946), 'Lord Keynes and the General Theory', *Econometrica*, 14/3, pp. 187–200.

Samuelson, Paul A. (1983), 'Thünen at Two Hundred', *Journal of Economic Literature*, 21, pp. 1468–88.

Schäfer, Annette (2008), *Die Kraft der schöpferischen*

Zerstörung: Joseph A. Schumpeter. Die Biographie (Frankfurt and New York: Campus).

Schmölders, Günter (1930), *Die Prohibition in den Vereinigten Staaten – Triebkräfte und Auswirkungen des amerikanischen Alkoholverbots* (Leipzig: Hirschfeld).

Schmölders, Günter (1988). *'Gut durchgekommen?' Lebenserinnerungen* (Berlin: Duncker & Humblot).

Schulze, Eberhard (2001), *Alexander Wassiljewitsch Tschajanow – die Tragödie eines großen Agrarökonomen* (Kiel: Vauk) (More in: *Sel'skij mir: Ėnciklopedija Rossijskich Dereven*, Agrarnyi Institut, Moscow, 1998.)

Sinn, Hans-Werner (2017), 'What Marx means today', CESifo Working Paper Series 6463.

Skidelsky, Robert (2004), *John Maynard Keynes 1883–1946: Economist, Philosopher, Statesman* (London: Pan Books).

Stark, W. (1941), 'Liberty and Equality or: Jeremy Bentham as an Economist', *The Economic Journal*, 51/201, pp. 56–79.

Thünen, Johann Heinrich von (2011), *Briefe* (Marburg: Metropolis).

Thünen, Johann Heinrich von (2013), *Zitate* (Dülmen: Laumann).

Tsokos, Michael (2009), *Dem Tod auf der Spur* (Berlin: Ullstein).

Varoufakis, Yanis (2015), 'How I became an erratic Marxist', https://www.theguardian.com/news/2015/feb/18/yanis-varoufakis-how-i-became-an-erratic-marxist.

Vickrey, William (1963), 'Pricing in Urban and Suburban

Transport', *American Economic Review,* 53/2, (Papers and Proceedings) pp. 452–65.

Vickrey, William (1994), *Public Economics: Selected Papers by William Vickrey* (Cambridge: Cambridge University Press).

Vickrey, William (1996), 'The Corporate Income Tax in the U.S. Tax System', *Tax Notes,* 73 (4/11/1996), pp. 597–604.

Vickrey, William (1997), 'A Trans-Keynesian Manifesto (Thoughts about an Asset-Based Macroeconomics)', *Journal of Post Keynesian Economics,* 19, pp. 495–510.

Vickrey, William (1998), 'Fifteen Fatal Fallacies of Financial Fundamentalism: A Disquisition on Demand-Side Economics', *Proceedings of the National Academy of Sciences of the United States of America,* 95, pp. 1340–47.

Vonderach, Gerd (2004), *Land-Leben gestern und heute* (Münster: Lit-Verlag).

Weizsäcker, Carl Christian von (2015), 'Kapitalismus in der Krise? Der negative natürliche Zins und seine Folgen für die Politik', *Perspektiven der Wirtschaftspolitik,* 16, pp. 189–212.

Weizbacher, Christian (2011), *Der radikale Narr des Kapitals* (Berlin: Matthes & Seitz).

Björn Frank, born in 1964, is Professor of Economic Theory at the University of Kassel. He is the author of many academic publications and several popular economics books, as well as two children's books. His most recent publication was the financial crime novel *Geldgerinnung* (with Johann Graf Lambsdorff, UVK Verlag, 2017).